100 MYTHS OF ENTREPRENEURSHIP VS. CHAINSAW

CUTTING THROUGH THE LIES STANDING
BETWEEN YOU AND
A MILLION DOLLAR BUSINESS.

JOSH SPURRELL, CPA

100 Myths of Entrepreneurship Vs. Chainsaw

ISBN 978-1-7778844-0-6

Copyright © 2021 by Josh Spurrell, CPA

Josh Spurrell Professional Corporation

Published by Josh Spurrell Professional Corporation
10207 111 St. NW
Edmonton, AB CA T5K 2V6

Josh Spurrell Professional Corporation books may be purchased for educational, business or sales promotional use. For more information, please email info@spurrell.ca. And visit spurrell.ca

CONTENTS

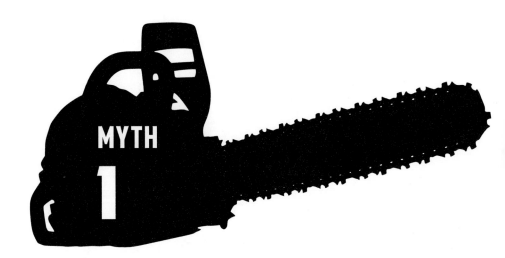

"You're going to go through
a time where you're not
going to make any money.
It's not going to be a week,
it's not going to be a month,
it's not going to be one
year. It's going to be years.
And during that time, if you
don't love what you do, it's
going to be very hard to
stick it out."

– GARY VAYNERCHUK

EVERYONE SHOULD START A BUSINESS SOMEDAY

*"96% of businesses fail within
10 years." – Forbes*

I have been studying, operating, and advising small businesses for more than 20 years now. Unlike video games, businesses do not have reset buttons. Failing at business often has catastrophic consequences on your personal finances, family relationships, and mental heath. Although I care deeply about small business owners, I am certainly not the hugging type. Yet too often, I have found myself trying to console the entrepreneur whose life is crashing down around them, wishing I had more of a huggable personality.

Tai Lopez's YouTube videos will make you think being an entrepreneur is a life of exotic cars, bikini clad women, and private jets. Business school makes you think that being an entrepreneur is a life of eloquent mission statements, market research, and perfect cash flow forecasts.

Starting a business is more like stepping into the octagon as an MMA fighter. You are going to get punched in the mouth, it is just a matter of when. Things will not go according to plan. People will get mad at you, lie, steal, break promises, and leave without warning. Owning a business is not for everyone just like being an MMA fighter is not for everyone. Reading this book will not change that. In fact, if I do not talk someone out of starting a business with this book, I would be failing at my life's mission of helping businesses beat the odds.

Most people are likely better off getting a good job, controlling their spending, and making smart investments over time. It is my experience that you are more likely to become a millionaire with this tried-and-true strategy.

However, for those who dare, this book is about turning you into the action hero in your own small business blockbuster movie. You know the character I am talking about. At some point in the movie their clothes are in tatters, their arm is in a sling, and they have blood trickling down their face. Yet somehow, they are still standing! I can not stop the pain that will inevitably come with entrepreneurship with this book, I can only prepare you to endure. Only if you remain standing long enough, will you have a chance to experience the benefits of entrepreneurship, like doing work that matters, financial freedom, and time freedom. Are you ready? If you plan to continue reading, I suggest a mouth guard!

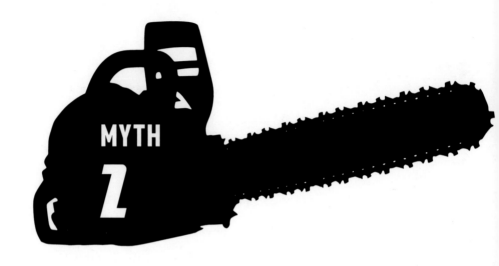

"Most people are wrong
about most things about
business, most of the time".
- CLAY CLARK

A LOT OF PEOPLE ARE KNOWLEDGEABLE ABOUT BUSINESS

"There are only 4 businesses for every 100 people." – Industry Canada

When I first heard that quote, I initially chuckled. Finally, I had a catchy line to summarize my rebuttals for every piece of bad business advice that clients bring to me. Often, these business grenades materialize after a client reads a blog written by someone hypothesizing online, about something they have never actually done, or after a client engages in a mastermind session with uncle their uncle Ron, who has been a union employee for the last 28 years.

Although I know this is going to hurt some feelings, we can not deposit feelings at the bank, so let us do some math. If we start with 5,000 people, we could estimate that 4% of those, or 200 out of 5,000 people, are entrepreneurs. Only 4% of those, or 8 out of 5,000 people, are entrepreneurs, that last 10 years or more. Only 50% of those, or 4 out of 5,000 people, are entrepreneurs, that last 10 years or more, that figure out how to scale to 5 employees or more. Only 50% of those, or 2 out of 5,000 people, figure out how to build a business valuable enough to be sold. Only 50% of those, or 1 out of 5,000 people, build a business worth a million dollars or more. Thus, the odds of building a million-dollar business, is in line with the odds of a 5-year-old boy, currently playing minor hockey, to end up playing 400 games or more in the NHL.

Thus, I have developed a filter that I would encourage business owners to follow. I only take business advice from people who have been in business for more than 10 years with 5 or more employees. These people are entrepreneurial unicorns and when you get a chance to hear them speak, you should listen!

Your uncle Ron, as much as you love him, does not count. It is not just Uncle Ron giving you bad advice. I am also not interested in the opinions of business school professors who have never actually walked the path. Government employees working at entrepreneurial resource centers are usually worse than the business school professors. Lawyers, bankers, and even accountants who have not scaled a business of their own, also, do not pass the sniff test.

You would likely learn more about business from a plumber who has built a 10-person plumbing business over the last 20 years, than someone in a fancy office who has only read books about building a business. Business is a contact sport. You can not learn it or become proficient in it from books alone. You must get on the field!

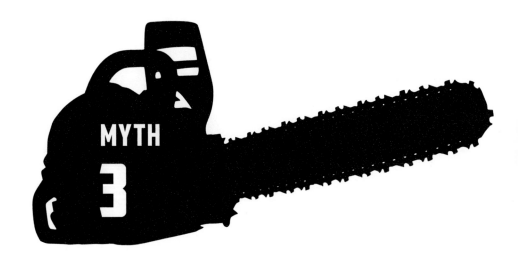

"The business schools
reward difficult complex
behavior more than simple
behavior, but simple
behavior is more effective."
– WARREN BUFFET

A BUSINESS DEGREE WILL PREPARE YOU TO OWN A BUSINESS

"Only 4.7% of recent university graduates start a business." – The Guardian

Previously I provided a harsh but effective filter, whereby you should ignore all business advice from those who have not run a business for more than 10 years and those who have not grown to 5 employees or more. This filter will cause you to ignore the advice from the more than 99% of the population who have never successfully walked the entrepreneurial path. This filter makes no exception for professors and instructors at business schools, who have not walked that path, nor should it.

I was asked by my local business college to speak to students on entrepreneurship. As my mission is to "help businesses beat the odds", I graciously accepted the appointment for free and booked times for an entire year. However, one day at a seminar I was asked a polarizing question. The student wanted to start a business and was wondering if they should continue their schooling or drop out to start their business immediately.

Knowing full well that the administration would not agree, I answered truthfully. I told them that business degrees are designed to prepare you to work in businesses and not run them. I pointed out that most of the instructors at business schools are career employees or entrepreneurs who need to supplement their income because of their lack of success. Therefore, the only reason to continue with a degree is because you are planning for your business to fail and you want something to fall back on. Shortly thereafter, my future scheduled events were cancelled by the school. Why would I take such a controversial position?

I have found that the way an entrepreneur organizes their calendar will often determine their likelihood for success. However, business schools never show you the calendar of successful business owners. Additionally, you can get a degree without ever generating even 1 lead from real marketing. You can get a business degree without ever selling something to a paying customer. The complex cash flow forecasting taught in business schools, ignores the fact that real world businesses will rarely qualify for the hypothetical loans proposed in the case studies. Also, the human resource tactics taught in business school are designed for someone whose only job within the company is human resources, not a busy entrepreneur.

Ultimately, these most basic and fundamental functions of running a business are not taught in business school. I can only attribute 10% of my knowledge that I apply everyday to my business degree and professional CPA training. The other 90% comes from real world experience and self study. Thus, in absence of a regulatory requirement, I cannot support a degree as a gateway to entrepreneurship, especially if student loans are required.

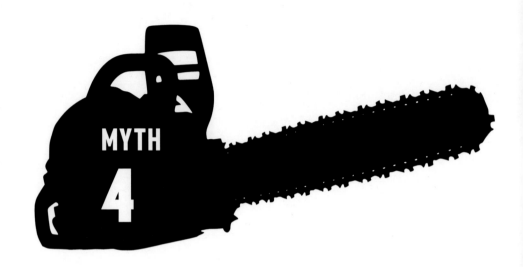

"If you really want to
dominate the competition
and make big bucks, you've
got to be the best. Do that,
be that, and no one will be
able to touch you. With one
exception. Someone with
less passion and talent and
poorer content can totally
beat you if they're willing
to work longer and harder
than you are. Hustle is it."
– GARY VAYNERCHUK

THAT YOU ARE SPECIAL

86% of franchises are still in business
after 5 years. – Franchise 101 Inc.

We now know that despite the efforts of the supposedly all-knowing business schools that 9 out of 10 businesses fail. Yet I run into entrepreneurs who end up starting multiple successful businesses. It is almost as if everything they touch turns to gold. For contrast we can also look at franchises, where 86% of franchises are still in business after 5 years. Most of these franchises are hardly unique. They provide seemingly mundane services like making pizza, dry-cleaning, and providing a gym to work out at.

How is it that we have some business owners that succeed repeatedly in various industries and franchises that make millions without a revolutionary idea in sight? I blame what I like to call the "participation ribbon bad artwork on the fridge unique snowflake fallacy".

Modern education reinforces the idea that people should get ribbons just for trying. It reinforces that all your crappy artwork should be put on the fridge. It teaches us that individuality, regardless of competence, should not just be tolerated but celebrated.

The problem is that this mentality makes you think that you can out create and outsmart other businesses. In other words, most business owners think that they are the next Henry Ford, Steve Jobs, or Mark Zuckerberg. When in reality, the market demand for your unique idea is likely no greater than the market demand for the crappy artwork you use to put on the fridge as a child.

Meanwhile successful business owners and franchises assume they have the creativity of a caveman. Rather than figure out how to make fire or build a wheel, they just copy how the other cavemen do it. Successful business owners often the draw on principles from other industries, but they rarely venture out into the unproven.

Rather than come up with the best marketing strategy ever, they just look at other successful marketing tactics and copy them. Rather than trying to be unique each time they provide their service, they write checklists. Rather than solving over complicated problems for their customers, they solve basic problems and focus all their efforts on out executing simple proven strategies. This breed of entrepreneur is a dangerous competitor. Rather than spending their time justifying their ego and their new way of doing things, they take the ideas already proven in the most successful businesses on the planet and focus on implementing and refining with maniacal focus.

"If your business depends on you, you don't own a business – you have a job. And it's the worst job in the world because you're working for a lunatic!"
– MICHAEL GERBER

THAT YOUR BUSINESS IS DIFFERENT

"A survey of failed entrepreneurs revealed that 42% of entrepreneurs who failed, report lack of customers as the most common primary reason for failure. 29% of entrepreneurs who failed, reported running out of cash as one of the primary reasons for failure, making it number 2. In third place, 23% of entrepreneurs who failed, reported not having the right team as one of the primary reasons for failure. The statistical relevance of all the other reasons for failure, such as, pricing, cost, timing, location, legal issues, paled in comparison to any of the top 3 reasons." – CB Insights

The overwhelming majority of business issues I tackle with clients could be categorized into one of the 3 common pain points. Lack of customers, lack of cash, or lack of quality team members. After working with thousands of entrepreneurs over the last 2 decades, successful entrepreneurs deploy proven strategies to predictably resolve these pain points. Unsuccessful entrepreneurs tend to tackle problems as if every business issue is like humankinds first trip to Mars.

They inevitably arrive at a strategy which they feel is unique, but likely has just shown to have a lower success rate.

Yet when I see entrepreneurs going down a dangerous path and attempt to educate them, they often come up with a common defense, "you don't understand my business". This line has become like fingernails on a chalkboard. It is like hearing someone say they drive better when they are drunk or that the world is flat.

They forget in the last couple of decades, I have worked with 1,000's of entrepreneurs in almost every industry imaginable. On multiple occasions, I have met with different clients in similar industries, in back-to-back meetings. One client will be making more than a million dollars per year and the next client in the same industry, will be struggling to pay rent. Yet when you try to coach the struggling client, they put up the common flailing defense, "you don't understand my business".

The harder concept for the average entrepreneur to grasp is that successful strategies tend to transcend industries. Although the professionals of the world may not like to hear it, when we analyze the business of a successful dentist and a successful plumber, they have much more in common than most would expect. As do the unsuccessful dentist and the unsuccessful plumber.

After all, business is all about solving 3 primary problems. Finding customers, not running out of cash, and building a good team. Therefore, successful entrepreneurs tend to succeed in multiple industries. Your business is not unique and once you understand that everything gets easier.

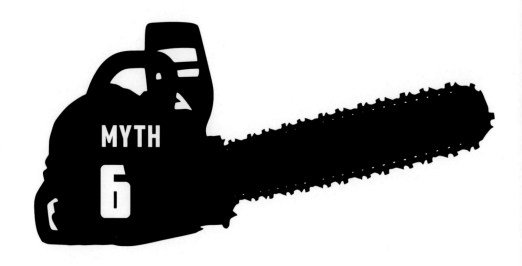

"The fatal assumption
is: if you understand
the technical work of a
business, you understand
a business that does that
technical work."
– MICHAEL GERBER

BEING A SPECIALIST IN YOUR FIELD QUALIFIES YOU TO RUN A BUSINESS IN THAT FIELD.

"Serial entrepreneurs generate 98% more sales than competitors." – Fast Company

Many new entrepreneurs I meet are starting a business in a field where they previously worked. Yet they struggle with the common pain points. While serial entrepreneurs, with no previous industry experience, replicate their success across industries.

I have met many brilliant accountants, who quote income tax law verbatim from memory that I did not know existed. Yet you look at their businesses and they fail to ever get 5 or more employees in their business. I am no longer shocked when their practice shuts down all together. After all, they do not teach us in business school how to launch a successful marketing campaign. They do not role play actual sales scenarios. Although accountants tend to have exceptional cash management skills, it is difficult to manage cash if you can not find customers. Moreover, no where along the way, do they give us the practical strategies to effectively recruit and develop employees, while simultaneously managing all other aspects of the business.

If an accountant's formal business training is inadequate when it comes to dealing with the 3 fundamental problems of business, what are the chances that med school prepares a doctor to run a business? What are the chances that trades school teaches a tradesman to run their business?

17

Given that 9 out of 10 businesses fail, it is safe to say that formal education is designed to allow you to work in that field, not run a business in that field.

I remember when I started my CPA practice, I had no idea how much work it was to setup the templates required to generate professional level financial statements at scale. Although I was proficient in doing the high-level technical work to complete corporate tax returns, I did not know how to setup and use the online portal required to electronically file tax returns. Afterall, the administration team at my previous firm took care of that. Not only did I have to set it up, I had to systemize my firms processes for the workflow, recruit staff for the role, and then train them on the processes. I was lucky that I had already learned how to sell things to real customers in my previous construction business. Many experienced technicians are overwhelmed by having to learn the administration of the business and sales simultaneously, when they strike out on their own.

Learning entrepreneurship is a 4-year degree all by itself. Just remember you will likely have to learn the material while also working full-time, to pay the bills. If you do not have the humility to admit that your technical abilities in your field are entirely unrelated to the required business skills, you will likely become an unfortunate statistic.

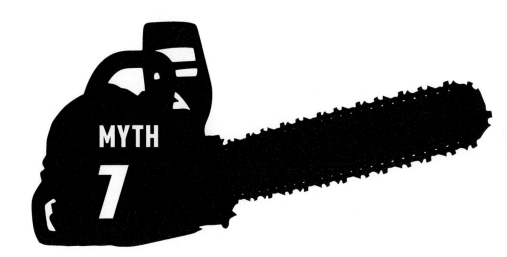

"Ideas are worthless
without the execution."
– GARY VAYNERCHUK

IDEAS ARE HARDER AND MORE IMPORTANT THAN EXECUTION

"The first company to sell a product in a new or resegmented market is 6 times more likely to fail than the companies that follow into the market." – Business Insider

Initial consults for new business owners are always fun. After all, I love businesses like most other people love babies or puppies. The business owner comes into the office with a special glimmer in their eye. Asking them about their idea is like asking someone who just got engaged about their special someone.

The new entrepreneur often proudly offers some facts quickly, like the size of the market and their industry knowledge. After doing thousands of these consults, I know that just like when you ask someone about their future spouse, business owners are usually excluding some details when talking about their business. After all, how could this CPA possibly understand this one-of-a-kind vision? Worse yet, what if the idea is so good that these people will steal my idea?

Despite the entrepreneur's conviction about a new idea, 90% will fail, and 30% will not even make it to year 2. As harsh as this rate of failure sounds, it is an overly optimistic stat for the rookie entrepreneur because successful businesses are often started by experienced entrepreneurs who start business after business with very few failures.

I have seen the best ideas with worldly knowledge, exceptional technology, and abundant customer demand fail because of poor execution. Yet I see people who make millions by effectively executing pedestrian ideas such as cleaning carpets and painting walls. A million-dollar idea only needs 2 components. A problem to solve and people willing to pay to solve that problem.

From there it is all about execution. Usually, execution over decades. Regardless of how exciting the initial idea was, a certain amount of monotony should be expected. Even the most unique ideas will leverage time tested tactics. Just because you are launching a new technology does not mean you should ignore proven marketing, cash flow, and human resource strategies.

Unsuccessful entrepreneurs often develop shiny object syndrome. Always wishing to create rather than execute. Successful entrepreneurs make small adjustments far more often than they pivot. They start as soon as possible with the minimal viable product required to generate income. Then they take pride in making their product or service just a little bit better each day. They use resistance as a motivation to keep going rather than an excuse to look for an easier path. Every employee who quits, every bad review, every customer who finds an excuse to not pay, becomes fuel for the fire rather than a sign that things are not working.

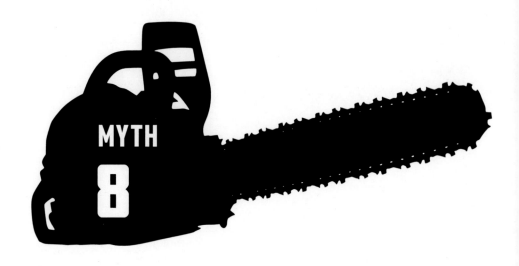

"If you are not willing to
learn, no one can help you.
If you are determined to
learn, no one can stop you."
– ZIG ZIGLAR

THAT SUCCESSFUL ENTREPRENEURS MAKE IT WITHOUT COACHING

"Business coaching has an average return on investment of 5.7 times the cost of the coaching." – The Manchester Review

By nature, most entrepreneurs are stubborn. After decades of working with entrepreneurs, the connection between entrepreneurs' natural uncoachable disposition and the high failure rate of small business, becomes obvious.

Hockey star Connor McDavid, basketball star Lebron James, and soccer star Lionel Messi all have coaches. Intuitively most people would project that despite their worldly abilities, that the teams these stars play on would likely underperform without a coach. I believe some would challenge how the value of coaching in team sports relates to entrepreneurship as many see entrepreneurship as more of an individual sport. However, then you would be left trying to explain why sports stars who do not play team sports, like tennis star Rafael Nadal, boxer Manny Pacquiao, or golf star Rory McIlroy, all choose to hire coaches. All these individuals were at one time the best in the world at their sport, yet they chose to hire external coaching to help them win.

I already know what you are thinking. Coaching works in sports not in business. I get it, I was a stubborn entrepreneur who knew everything once too. Then I learned that Jeff Bezos, Steve Jobs, Sergey Bryn, and Larry Page all had a business coach. What really blew my mind was they all used the same coach, Bill Campbell. Then it became clear to me if you want to be a hack shooting hoops outside your garage, you do no have to worry about a coach. However, if you want to win at sports or in business, hire a coach!

Personally, I am surrounded by coaches and business consultants in our group of companies. However, people inside the organization tend to suffer from group think and tunnel vision. Plus, it is difficult for an employee who relies on their pay cheques as their sole means to provide for their family, to critique the boss. It takes someone outside the organization to get that 30,000-foot overview and provide objective feedback. Thus, just like Jeff Bezos, I meet with an external business coach weekly to get analysis that is not obvious from the inside and hold me accountable to progress on strategic milestones.

The allure of entrepreneurship and coaching are at all time highs. There is a plethora of well-read individuals who might even have had a degree of success in an executive role, who woke up one day and decided they are business coaches. However, statistically speaking, individuals who founded million-dollar businesses are extremely rare. They are unicorns. It is my experience that these unicorns have business acumen that will allow success in varying industries. I strongly recommend a coach who is a "unicorn" or someone who works for a "unicorn" in a professional coaching business.

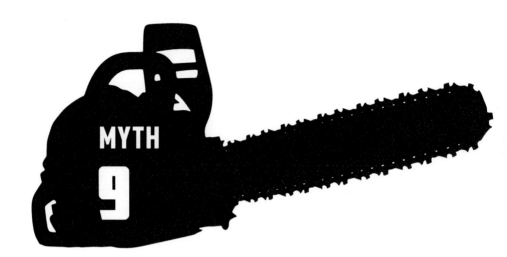

"Your time is limited, so don't waste it living someone else's life. Don't be trapped by dogma - which is living with the results of other people's thinking. Don't let the noise of other's opinions drown out your own inner voice. And most important, have the courage to follow your heart and intuition. They somehow already know what you truly want to become. Everything else is secondary."

– STEVE JOBS

THAT YOUR BUSINESS WILL NOT AFFECT YOUR PERSONAL LIFE

"72% of entrepreneurs report mental health issues." – Forbes

I recently had a husband-and-wife team who were trying to grow their side hustle into a fulltime business. However, as time passed, I noticed they were not completing their strategic initiatives on their business plan. As I suspected, their revenue numbers were not increasing, and they were not getting any closer to realizing their dreams of being fully self employed. When it came to personal tax time, they had a renewed sense of vigour in communicating with our office. Unfortunately, they were not looking for assistance with knocking out their strategic initiatives, they were looking for special help in claiming their recreational cannabis use.

Turns out they are active in the cannabis community. They attend events, have an active social life with friends in the community, and ultimately spend a significant amount of time enjoying cannabis. The difficult conversation that was required here is to tell them that their lifestyle is in direct conflict with their entrepreneurial goals.

Now the natural inclination would be to assume that this opinion is based solely on a moral judgement of that lifestyle. However, that assumption misses the bigger issue here. Although I have no interest in cannabis, I use to have interest in playing men's league hockey and slo-pitch. Even though these activities are less morally divisive, they were just as detrimental to my entrepreneurial journey.

I learned that successful entrepreneurs do not actually have more ability than unsuccessful ones, they are just focusing their efforts on fewer goals. They have less variety in their life, especially in the growth phase of their business. Most successful entrepreneurs who have kids likely have very few other interests other than their business and their family.

This lack of variety is not for everyone. However, successful entrepreneurs are not maintaining this narrow focus through extreme will power. They become addicted to being great at a few things rather than dabbling in many. Eventually hanging out with a bunch of slow pitch players, half of whom are likely unwilling to dive after a ball to win the game, becomes boring when compared to crushing your business competitors. Ultimately, it is not going to be about work life balance. It is going to be about work life trade offs and the trade offs required to avoid becoming a statistic will change your personal life dramatically. Those not prepared to make those trade offs are likely not prepared to succeed at entrepreneurship.

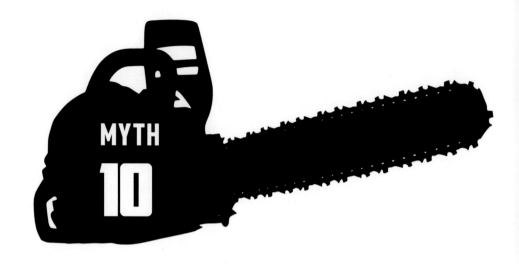

"Have the conversation with the person
that's holding you back. The reason
most people who are listening right
now are not doing that thing, is that
they are worried about the opinion
of somebody. Usually, their mother.
Usually, their father and the reality is
that your spouse may be the person
holding you back and you have to have
that conversation. We have to get to the
place where you are doing you because
the number one thing that scares the
f*ck out of me is regret and you're
gonna sit here at 72 and you're gonna
say I wish, I wish, I wish"

- GARY VAYNERCHUK

THAT FAMILY & FRIENDS WILL BE ABLE TO AGREE OR RELATE TO LIFE AS AN ENTREPRENEUR.

*"63% of people want to start a
business someday." – Inc.com*

It is unlikely that any of your family or friends, who are not dentists, will offer advice on how to perform your own root canal. However, most of them will likely give you business advice. Why is that? It is because 63% of people want to start a business someday. Thus, most people in your life are going to have an opinion about how you should run your business because in their heads, they are entrepreneurs.

However, as roughly only 1 in 5,000 people have built a million-dollar business, getting business advice from friends and family, is likely as dangerous as amateur root canals. I cannot count the number of times a business owner will come into my office and justify a business decision that's likely to take them off a cliff with the words "I have talked it over with my family and I'm going to ....".

Running a business is kind of like being a fire fighter. Most people run out of the building when it is on fire, but firefighters run into it. The things you must do to win at business are often at odds with the cultural norms we have been taught from an early age. We are taught 40 hours is a normal work week, yet successful entrepreneurs work more. We are taught to expect a guaranteed wage, yet successful entrepreneurs take risks for the mere chance at profits. We are taught that a penny saved is a penny earned, yet successful entrepreneurs pay people to help them save time whenever practical. We are taught that word of mouth is the most noble of all marketing tactics, yet the business who spends the most on marketing usually wins. We are taught that relationships last forever, yet entrepreneurs who plan for inevitable staff turnover avoid staffing issues.

I am not advocating turning your back on your family and friends. You simply must take their recommendations as a sign of affection, rather than sound strategy that has a reasonable chance at success. After all, many entrepreneurs are running a business to provide for those important to them. However, if you want to succeed at that goal, you are going to have make decisions, without any reassurance of consensus support from those you love.

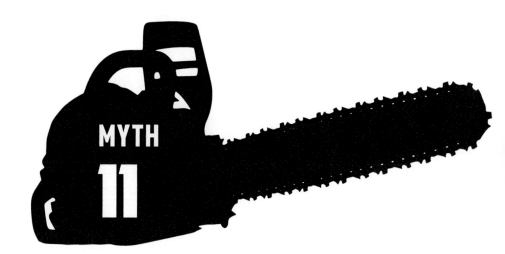

"The 3 C's of Life: Choices,
Chances, Changes. You
must make a choice to take
a chance or your life will
never change."
– ZIG ZIGLAR

THERE ARE RISK FREE OPTIONS.

"From the beginning of 2015 to the end of 2019 McDonalds had losses relating to closing of under-performing restaurants totalling $74 million dollars." – McDonalds Annual Reports

Did you know Steve Jobs was fired from his own company? Did you know Henry Ford failed at 2 car companies before gaining success with the Ford Motor Company? Did you know Walt Disney filed for bankruptcy after launching his first film studio? Did you know Sam Walton's landlord gained control of his first store when his lease expired?

We are taught in school that there are right and wrong answers. The fear of being wrong is routed deep within our upbringing. Thus, I get clients who agonize over decisions. Yet, we see throughout history, successful people that were willing to make mistakes. What can we learn from this?

Firstly, entrepreneurs should recognize that the volume of decisions they will encounter is immense. Think of a 100-question multiple choice test. If you agonize over question 1 you may increase the likelihood of coming up with a better solution, but you will still fail miserably because you did not address the other 99 decisions in a timely manner. The most successful entrepreneurs are not right all the time, they simply make enough good decisions to matter.

Secondly, we should realize that not all decisions matter equally. Some will have significant impacts, and some will have very minor impacts. Entrepreneurs should allocate their time according.

Thirdly, you should identify options that have catastrophic risks and avoid them as often as possible. Although you may have to go "all in" at times, successful businesses are usually built on being right more often than not on a series of small decisions. In baseball terms, successful entrepreneurs focus on hitting singles everyday rather than risking a strikeout for a potential homerun.

Finally, and probably the most difficult conventional mindset to overcome, is that potential benefits cannot be considered in a binary win or loss. Even if the probability of success for a decision is low, if the benefit is significant enough, it is worth taking the risk. For example, suppose you identify an advertising initiative that will cost $30,000 per year. Let us say you have a $100,000 in operating capital so regardless of the outcome the risk is not catastrophic. If it works, you could potentially generate an additional $300,000 in profit, or a 10x return on your investment. Even if the probability for success is only 25%, prudent entrepreneurs make this investment all day long, whereas conventional education suggests getting hung up on the odds being less than 50%.

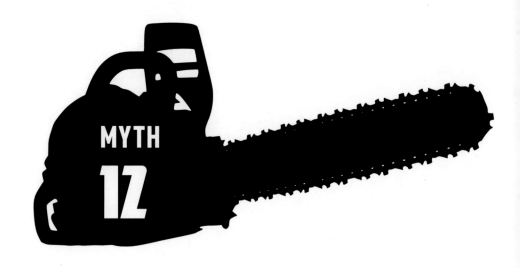

"Most people who fail in their dream, fail not from lack of ability, but from lack of commitment."

– ZIG ZIGLAR

THAT YOU CAN BUILD A SUSTAINABLE BUSINESS OR MAKE MAJOR CHANGES IN 1 YEAR.

"65% of businesses viable enough to be listed for sale have been around for more than 5 years and 50% of businesses viable enough to be listed for sale have been around for more than 10 years." - Forbes

Often, I will have clients come for an initial consult and they have next to no revenue today but believe they will have 7-figure revenue in the first year or two. Sometimes they feel one of the most important components to discuss in the initial meeting for their baby business, is their exit strategy. Inevitably the first-year end will come for these happy hopers and there will be little revenue to speak of. They will usually still latch on to 1 or 2 issues that they believe to be responsible for the lack of rocket ship like growth. One year out they will usually be able to delude themselves into thinking that they are still on the brink of breaking through to explosive growth any day. Then we meet to review the financial performance for year 2 and reality usually begins to set in.

I understand the mentality. After all, when you read business articles it appears that every successful entrepreneur was an overnight success. When you dig deeper you find that most were overnight successes decades in the making. Sure, there are exceptions to this rule. However, attaching your dreams to this type of success model is mathematically no different than attempting to achieving success by winning the lottery.

By changing your time horizon, you can flip the odds in your favour. Stop thinking about homeruns and start thinking about the most probable way to get to first base. Often it involves reducing personal expenditures and launching a minimal viable product that will pay the bills even if nothing else goes your way.

A lot of people look at that model and think that it conflicts with achieving their long-term vision because the first step looks drastically different then their long-term goal. However, the difference between successful and unsuccessful entrepreneurs is rarely vision. It is execution. It is continually making a lot of small but important choices over time and getting them right more often than not. Then once you have honed that decision-making muscle and battle tested it through the years, you make more significant decisions. Sometimes your vision will change for the better along the way. Sometimes it will remain the same. In either case, you are more likely to achieve that vision by playing the long game.

Reputation takes a long time to build. Top of mind awareness among likely buyers takes time. Cash reserves take time to build. Business credit and investor confidence takes time. The best teams are built with time not money. Thus, if you change your time horizon your chances of success increase exponentially. Business is a game that is played over decades not months.

"There's no such thing as
perfect. Chasing perfect'
is the shortest road to not
achieving it."
- GARY VAYNERCHUK

THAT BEING A PERFECTIONIST IS A PROFITABLE TRAIT.

"Amazon spent $22.6 billion in research and development in 2018, more than any other company on earth. Then on January 7, 2019 they became the worlds largest company." – Statista.com

To put this in perspective, there are approximately 90 billion countries in the world who have a gross domestic product of less than $22.6 billion. Any company who spends this much money on improving their products and services does not do so because they believe their existing offering is perfect. Where would Amazon be today if Jeff Bezos would have waited to launch Amazon in a perfect office space instead of launching in his garage?

When hiring, we often hear from candidates that they feel their biggest weakness is that they are a perfectionist. They think it is the "perfect" answer. However, now when I hear this, I just assume this is a person who misses deadlines. After all, there is no such thing as perfect, but it turns out, completing a task is powerful.

I often see businesses burning through cash with their first hopes of revenue months away. Yet, I find most successful entrepreneurs look back on their first iterations of their product or service with embarrassment. Then they use profits and experience to make improvements over time, to become better at their craft. Ultimately, to arrive at a destination that was wholly impossible at the start.

In the businesses I have launched, if someone would have given me a blank cheque and allowed me to perfect my first service offering prior to generating revenue, I would likely be further behind then where I am today. I would have invariably wasted time overthinking. More importantly, I would have overemphasized the importance of my own beliefs and underestimated market feedback. Market feedback that only comes when you start selling real things to real people.

Perfection is in fact the enemy, not a virtue. Successful businesses are built on measuring and adjusting in perpetuity, in search of improvement, not perfection.

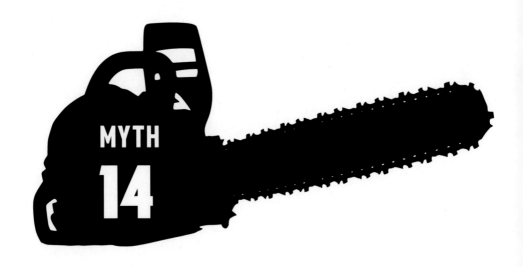

MYTH 14

"The test is not a complex one: when the alarm goes off, do you get up out of bed, or do you lie there in comfort and fall back to sleep? If you have the discipline to get out of bed, you win— you pass the test. If you are mentally weak for that moment and you let that weakness keep you in bed, you fail. Though it seems small, that weakness translates to more significant decisions. But if you exercise discipline, that too translates to more substantial elements of your life." **– JOCKO WILLINK**

YOU CAN AVOID THE FUNCTIONS OF THE BUSINESS YOU DON'T LIKE

"54% of businesses have 4 employees
or less." – Industry Canada

In working with entrepreneurs, we find most people who start businesses are overly focused on the technical aspects of their business. Falsely, they assume that if they focus solely on doing the technical aspects of their business well, that word of mouth referrals will eventually take care of everything else. They view entrepreneurship as a means to have complete autonomy. Thus, allowing them to execute a constantly evolving service offering at their sole discretion, instead of having to listen to a boss.

However, this is not how businesses scale. Running a successful business is about developing a set of repeatable processes to deliver products and services that solve problems for the purchaser. In order to scale, you have to allocate ongoing time to marketing, sales, documenting processes, recruiting, training, coaching, accounting, and administration.

Most entrepreneurs we meet do not like one or more of these functions. They falsely assume that an exceptional skill set in one of these areas will overcome their lack of attention to another. Inevitably ignoring any one of these functions for a prolonged period will result in one of the 3 primary problems of business ... not enough customers, not enough cash, and not having the right team.

41

Occasionally a business owner will think they can hire someone to absolve them of one of these responsibilities. However, the difference between abdication and delegation is minor to the untrained eye, the result is often drastically different. Delegation involves establishing specific quantifiable goals, measuring the performance, and course correcting when necessary. While abdication almost always results in significant failure. The only question becomes when.

Moreover, as most businesses have limited start-up funds, the functions that should be delegated also need to be limited. Although this triggers uncomfortable work, it results in increased knowledge which will be beneficial when you eventually have to supervise delegated work in the future. Moreover, the effect of demonstrating to team members a willingness to do the work that needs doing, rather than the work that you enjoy, creates a valuable culture of discipline.

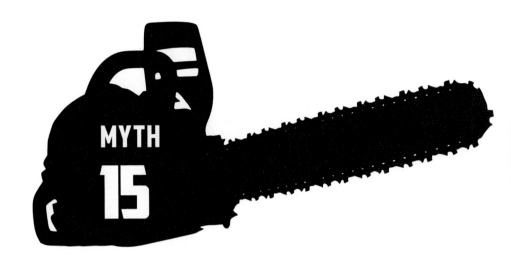

"Don't expect to be
motivated every day to get
out there and make things
happen. You won't be. Don't
count on motivation. Count
on Discipline"
– JOCKO WILLINK

YOU CAN WORK WHEN YOU FEEL MOTIVATED

"Only 14% of all franchises are out of business in 5 years." – Franchise 101 Inc.

Generally, the business plans we generate for clients at our firm have strategic milestones with dates attached. The milestones include things like, optimizing a Google business listing, creating a YouTube channel, launching a recruiting ad, etc. However, too often we meet with the client the following year to update the plan and find that many of the strategic initiatives are not complete.

Society continually promotes the narrative that discomfort is unhealthy. How many times have you heard that working less will make you happier and healthier? Yet as the hours in the average workweek decrease, the rates of depression and anxiety increase.

I believe we have forgotten our primal roots. After all, we survived for millions of years by gathering food and avoiding predators. It was not easy. Thus, waiting for motivation while we exist in a comfortable environment goes against our evolutionary origins. We have to act first, and the sense of accomplishment generally comes after.

This is one of the reasons why franchise businesses succeed at higher rates than non-franchise businesses. It is not because the franchise business owners are more motivated crowd then their non-franchise counterparts. The franchise business owners are equipped with a simple set of proven steps to execute regardless of how they feel. No step on its own being remarkable. However, when executed with diligence and consistency over time, result in a high probability of success.

The next time you feel apprehensive about tackling an uncomfortable task, remember, that the voices in your head preaching comfort, is just social conditioning perpetrated by people who did not create successful businesses. People who run successful businesses develop the habit of heading towards resistance and difficult tasks. Once you start achieving success, your brain will start to equate the difficult task with the actual success you are pursuing. This results in entrepreneurs who often get a twisted sense of enjoyment out of being confronted with a difficult task. However, the apprehension to act prior to motivation will always linger and should generally be fought with massive action.

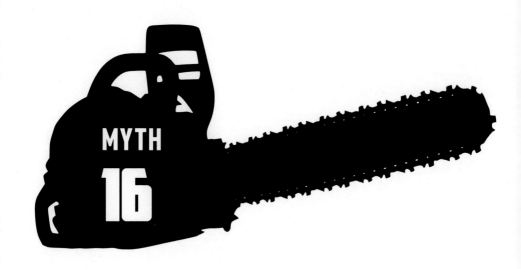

"Super-successful people aren't superhuman at all; they've just used selected discipline to develop a few significant habits. One at a time. Over time."

– GARY KELLER

THAT CUSTOMERS, SUPPLIERS, OR EMPLOYEES VALUE YOUR TIME

"Small business owners waste 21.8 hours each week." – Inc Magazine

Whether you are bootstrapping your business with no money or you have millions to grow your business, every entrepreneur gets the same 168 hours in the week.

Business owners often view time as an unlimited resource. This false truth is reinforced during the infancy stage of the business. As the demand is low and the teams are small, the business owner completes tasks that do not ad value without negatively affecting the business.

Then the business grows. The client who needs to be personally called every day becomes upset when they must wait a day for a call back. The supplier who can only communicate through never-ending email threads fails to deliver on time. The worker who needed constant oversight is left unattended and starts making mistakes. The business owner becomes confused as things start to slip away despite the same level of effort. They double down with more hours only to find that the 168-hour per week limit is firm, and self doubt begins to set in.

As you begin to scale your business you need to insist on certain boundaries on your time. It is no longer enough to make money on a customer, you have to be able to make money on a customer in a reasonable amount of time. It is no longer enough that a supplier has the technical abilities, they have to interact with you efficiently. It is no longer enough that your employees have minimal competencies, you need to surround yourself with employees who can grow into taking more and more responsibilities off your plate.

Ordinarily this will mean that some customers, suppliers, and employees who were a fit during the infancy of your business will no longer be a fit as your busines matures. We are preconditioned growing up to think that the breakdown of these relationships is a sign of failure, when in fact these transitions are a sign of growth. This should not be confused with moving on for the sake of moving on. As turnover, by itself, does not promote growth. Often, people who grow with you long term are your best assets. However, we must avoid time sucking relationships and protocols that are kept purely out of nostalgia.

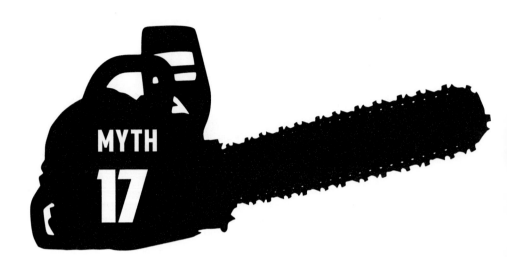

"The entrepreneurial model has less to do with what's done in a business and more to do with how it's done. The commodity isn't what's important – the way it's delivered is."

– MICHAEL GERBER

THAT MEETING CUSTOMERS EXPECTATIONS ARE GOOD ENOUGH

"7 out of 10 consumers say they've spent more money to do business with a company that delivers great service." – American Express

I routinely see entrepreneurs who attack entrepreneurship with a diligent employee mindset. They imagine their product or service agreement with a customer as a good employee would view their job description. They recommend minimal services to keep prices low. Then they deliver a product or service within those exact minimal specifications. Then the customer inevitably leaves for a cheaper alternative or provider who does more.

I try to teach entrepreneurs to provide products and services with more included benefits than their competitors. I teach them to concisely summarize these benefits versus their competitors on a single sheet that can be presented to the prospective customers. However, it should not stop there. You should always attempt to stack additional benefits into the actual product or service delivery, that would not even be practical to go through in a sales presentation. You want your product or service to be seen as having a unique value proposition rather than a replaceable homogenous commodity.

Often these benefits start right from the moment a potential customer reaches out. At this point you decide to present to them a capable person to book them into an appointment. Alternatively, you provide them a capable person, with contagious energy, armed with an array of solutions to put their minds at ease.

When they arrive at the office. Do you have stale coffee or a made fresh cappuccino? Do they have something to do in the waiting room? Do you give them gifts? Do you send them a generic Christmas card, or do you make a video collage of everyone on the team wishing them a Merry Christmas individually?

There will be technically focused dissenters out there who will say these ancillary things do not matter. However, if that were true 5-star hotels would go out of business overnight. All high-end restaurants would be closed in favor of fast-food chains. Finally, the Tiffany blue box would be replaced by Costco jewelry packaging. No matter your personal perception on the issue, the market has spoken. The market favours goods and services from providers who prioritize both presentation and the overall customer experience.

"Don't be distracted by
criticism. Remember the
only taste of success some
people have is when they
take a bite out of you."
– ZIG ZIGLAR

THAT EVERY CUSTOMER IS A GOOD CUSTOMER

"18.1% of the population are suffering from anxiety or depression at any given time."–
Anxiety and Depression Association of America

Often business owners will ask for my thoughts on changes they intend to make to their business because of customer feedback. When I ask them how often they have received similar feedback, I find they tend to be contemplating major adjustments for isolated events.

Conventional education and values suggest that the goal should be 100% customer satisfaction. However, conventional economics suggests that the customer will always want more for less and your employees always want to work less for more. Thus, the idea of a perfect product or service becomes a paradox. Moreover, as you improve your products and services, incremental improvements become more and more costly. The goal is to find customers that have realistic expectations for the price being charged.

Often if a reasonable customer was presented with the additional cost to deliver their idea for improvement, they would prefer to keep the product or service as is. We have all had our moments where our emotion interfered with logical decisions. Every reasonable person does. Thus, it should be expected that even reasonable customers will make unreasonable suggestions from time to time.

Then we have to consider the feedback from non-reasonable people. If we know over 18% of the population is in a state of dissatisfaction with their lives, what percentage of customers consistently make unrealistic demands? Although unrealistic customer demands are not as heavily studied as depression, I would suggest by eye those numbers are somewhat similar. Unfortunately, we also have the darker truth that there is a certain percentage of the population that commit heinous crimes. In parallel there are a certain percentage of customers who will advance their own self interest within business transactions without any consideration for fairness or even decency.

We need to understand in no uncertain terms that 100% customer satisfaction is a myth. I would suggest that 9 out of 10 is the standard of excellence we should pursue. Rather than pursuing perfection, the road to a profitable scalable business involves going the extra mile to overdeliver to reasonable customers and unloading unreasonable customers as quickly as possible.

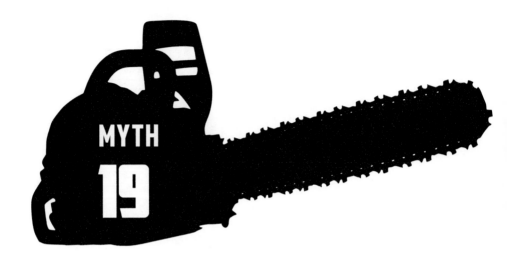

"A person's success
in life can usually be
measured by the number
of uncomfortable
conversations he or she is
willing to have."
– TIM FERRISS

THAT YOU CAN MAKE ANY SORT OF PROGRESS WITHOUT CONFLICT.

"The typical manager spends 25-40% of their time dealing with conflicts." – Forbes

In speaking with entrepreneurs, I find that a lot of businesses are started because the entrepreneur had a toxic relationship with their previous employer. The rational is that once they venture out on their own, they can avoid the stress of that relationship. Although the entrepreneur becomes free of that one relationship upon start-up, they usually find that the overall level of conflict increases as you interact with more and more people.

Unfortunately, entrepreneurs who grow to any scale find that people are often rude, leave without notice, lie, and sometimes flat out steal from you. To grow a busines larger and larger, you have to interact with more and more people. Thus, these troubling instances of conflict tend to increase with entrepreneurship rather than decrease.

This should not be misunderstood to believe that people who create and enjoy conflict make successful business owners. In fact, my experience would suggest the opposite. People who have success in business, long-term, tend to value building healthy relationships over time. Although short-term success can be had from a win at all cost attitude, long term success tends to be built on strong relationships built on win-win terms.

Yet, your ability to have difficult conversations is necessary to course correct relationships and steer them towards win-win terms. Thus, increasing the number of fruitful relationships. If the relationship is unmanageable with reasonable effort, the ability to terminate relationships will be necessary. Entrepreneurship is often like pruning a tree. You are constantly caring for the branches that align with the core and cutting out the relationships that do not fit.

If you are looking for less conflict on its own, I would suggest simply switching employers. However, if you are willing to tackle new conflicts head on in perpetuity, keep reading.

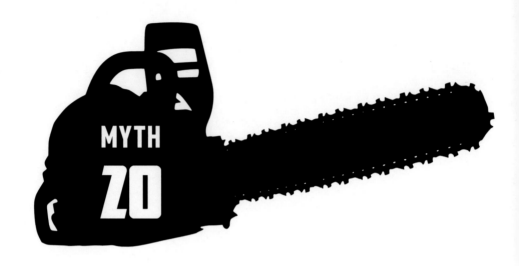

"People who are
exceptionally good in
business aren't so because
of what they know but
because of their insatiable
need to know more."
– MICHAEL GERBER

THAT YOU WILL EVER BE DONE LEARNING

"Only 11% of business owners seek professional help." - Intuit

I have found that the know-it-all personality type is attracted to entrepreneurship. Thus, it was not surprising to find out that roughly only 1 in 10 entrepreneurs ever hire a professional lawyer or accountant. In parallel 9 out of 10 business fail.... Let that sink in!

Unfortunately, I know professional accounting and legal advice, does not by itself guarantee success. As such, I must believe that these stats point out a bigger issue. The issue being that of the small percentage of the population who ever starts a business, a much smaller percentage has the humility to recognize that they must learn the unintuitive skill of business to succeed.

If you are one of the people who still has an inkling that you know-it-all, ask yourself who taught you? We are clearly not taught entrepreneurial principles growing up. Most conventional mindsets are rooted in an employee mindset. How many people do you know who have started a business? Who do you know that has been in business for more than 10 years? Who do you know who know who has more than 5 employees working for them? Who do you know that has ever sold a business? Who do you know that sold a business for more than $1,000,000?

I can tell you it is not taught in school. I have a business degree and a CPA designation. No one who was teaching me at school would have answered yes to all of the questions above. Rather they work for the University and they are teaching you how to work for a business, not own one.

I did not gain exponential business knowledge with my business degree. I learned incrementally over 2 decades by running, studying, and advising businesses. The only shortcut I have ever found has been the result of studying people more successful than me and implementing their formula. I do not mean hearing a quote and acting on the spirit of it. I mean replicating their exact sequence of steps to solve a problem. Once you realize that most of your ideas are ordinary, all you must do is copy proven strategies and execute them with more discipline than your competition. Then you become virtually unstoppable as a business owner.

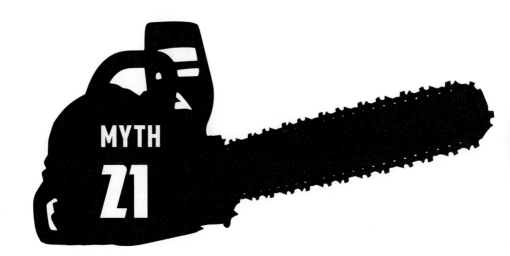

"Time on a task, over time,
eventually beats talent
every time."
– GARY KELLER

YOU CAN WORK 4 HOURS PER WEEK AND RUN A BUSINESS

"Entrepreneurs work on average 63%
more then employees." – RealBusiness.co

Another reason I find people start businesses is because they are unhappy with the number of hours they are working at their current job. Then they see a book about 4-hour work weeks, they see an Instagram post that makes entrepreneurship look like a travel blog, and they start to think that the quickest path to time freedom is to start a business.

Starting a successful business will normally require the entrepreneur to work the equivalent of working 2 different fulltime jobs. To succeed you will likely have to work the equivalent of 1 fulltime employee delivering the product or service and then find time to devote the equivalent of a second fulltime employee to work on the business.

I remember when I started my accounting firm. I knew how to do the work, but I was ill-prepared as an organization to deliver the service. I did not have my terms of engagement written out to formally engage with clients. Then once I had terms written out, I had to address the fact that I did not have a letterhead or, for that matter, a logo to put on the letter head. Then once I had the client signed up, I had to address that I did not have the fancy automated statements that save countless hours on preparing formal annual financial statements. Thus, I had to buy software and then pay a programmer to customize it for my firm. Then upon completing my first-year end, I was all ready to send the file to the administration department so they could electronically file it with the government. The only problem being, I was the administration department and my firm had not yet gone through the qualification process to electronically file years ends with the government.

I know some may think that these are one-time setup issues. However, the administration of the business is a forever task. Supplier contracts need to be renegotiated and new suppliers need to be sourced. Employees need feedback and departing employees need to be replaced. The business grows out of locations and equipment become obsolete. Remember the staff training sessions at your last job? It is now your job to stay current with all new regulations, best practices, and train everyone around you. Let us not forget about marketing and sales and more marketing and more sales.

I would suggest that in the absence of significant start-up capital, the minimum time requirement to build a successful business is 60+ hours per week. I don't mean 60+ hours a week for a few weeks, I mean 60+ hours for a few years! Anything less will dramatically decrease your chance of long-term success.

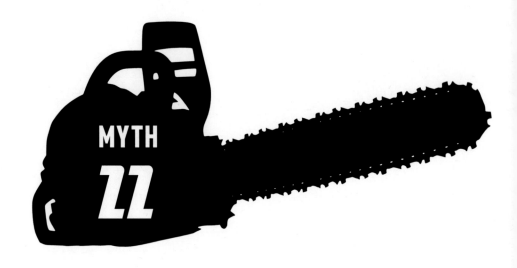

Discipline is the difference
between being good and
exceptional."
– JOCKO WILLINK

YOU CAN CHANGE YOUR SCHEDULE WHENEVER YOU FEEL LIKE IT

"72% of a CEO's time is spent in meetings."
– CNBC & Harvard Business Review

Throughout the years it has been interesting to see the contrasting behaviour of successful and unsuccessful clients. For example, successful clients rarely miss or reschedule meetings. While unsuccessful clients suffer from never endings unforeseen scheduling conflicts. Think of how difficult it is for a CEO to reschedule. I know if someone reschedules with me, I likely do not have any available time for another month or so.

Less seasoned entrepreneurs seem to think that they can work on being organized once they have made it. As if organization is an optimization exercise which takes something that is good and makes it great. They delude themselves into thinking that it is easy for successful business owners to have a regimented calendar because they have resources like assistants, cash flow, and automated marketing systems.

I am going to let you in on a secret from years of watching entrepreneurs, both successful and unsuccessful ones. Most successful entrepreneurs begin without resources. The resources they obtained were a result of implementing a regimented scheduled.

I equate changing your calendar with high interest payday loans. I will explain. Let us assume you have a 1-hour meeting with a supplier on your calendar. Then a customer issue arises, so you decide to reschedule the meeting to deal with the customer issue immediately. The problem is the meeting with the supplier, although seemingly less urgent, is still necessary to operate the business in the long term. Thus, you are going to engage in an email exchange back and forth or voicemails back and forth to reschedule the meeting in a week or so. Every correspondence creating an interruption which reduces your efficiency. Before you know it, you have given an additional 15 minutes of your time to reschedule the meeting. Effectively turning the 1-hour then time commitment today into a 1.25-hour commitment. That is no different than borrowing $1,000 today and paying back $1,250 the following week. However, time is more valuable than money. You can make more money, but your 168 hours per week is finite.

This issue further compounds because once you start asking people on your calendar to reschedule, they become more likely to ask you to return the favour sometime in the future. This goes beyond suppliers, as employees will start to feel that deadlines are flexible. It becomes a slippery slope that usually results in the entrepreneur missing the most important meetings, the ones with themselves. Usually resulting in replacing the time allocated to generate more customers with time spent on dealing with current customer needs. Thus, the doom loop of more and more time spent on increasingly needy customers begins.

"If you don't plan your
time, someone else will
help you waste it."
– ZIG ZIGLAR

UNSCHEDULED TASKS WILL GET DONE IN YOUR FREE TIME

"89% of people admit to wasting time at work." – Forbes

I find that most of the time when someone is struggling with an aspect of their business, it is because they do not have time in their calendar to address the issue. They want more customers, but they do not have any time carved out to do marketing. They want to get their finances in order, but they do not have time allocated to review their financial reports. They want a better team, but they do not have time allocated to recruit or train employees. Then they say the fatal words that usually sounds something like, "one of these weekends I will get to that".

The other issue tends to be allocating time only in spurts rather than on a permanent recurring basis. Let us think about the issues listed above. If you are reaching out to new perspective clients, it is not likely that they will do business with you if you call them once. However, if you call them once a month for a year, now you have a shot. The first time you look at your financials they will be a mess. Slowly you will clean them up over time with diligence. Then by reviewing them on a consistent periodic basis, you gain the ability to make better decisions based on up to date, accurate information. Finally, when it comes to building the team, you can not expect to whip underperforming employees into shape with one workshop. You develop employees over time.

You need to break down every aspect of your business including marketing, sales, production, administration, recruiting, and training. Each one of these functions should have permanent recurring time blocks on your calendar.

Once you plot everything out on a recurring weekly or monthly calendar, it starts to become clear the realistic time that can be allocated to each task. Normally the first few times through your calendar each block will seem somewhat inadequate and it will feel like you can not accomplish everything you want to accomplish. However, it forces you to avoid time sucking impossible pursuits of perfection. Ultimately ensuring you do not ignore any key component of the business. After all, you are never "finished" when it comes to any key area of your business. It is the incremental improvements overtime, on all key aspects of the business, that matter. Thus, your goal of each time block becomes to make the business just a little better than where it was at the start of that time block.

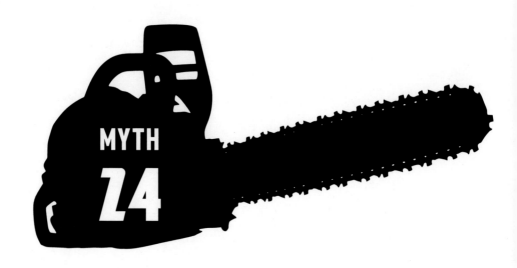

"Do your most important
work – your ONE thing –
early, before your willpower
is drawn down"
– GARY KELLER

YOU CAN SLEEP IN AND WORK LATER TO CATCH UP

"90% of executives wake up before 6AM on weekdays." – Huffington Post

I get entrepreneurs who tell me that they are not a morning person and that they are going to attempt to devise their calendar around their penchant for sleeping in. Unfortunately, late risers are put at a strategic disadvantage to their early rising counterparts.

Entrepreneurs love to pride themselves on their decision-making ability. However, just like a truck driver who increases their chance of an accident with each additional hour as fatigue sets in, so too does the entrepreneur temp fate making decisions as they become fatigued. Decision making is like any other physical human function that deteriorates as we fatigue. Thus, we are best served by organizing your day with the most important decisions and tasks done first.

Now, some will question why they simply can not tackle their important decisions first thing at 9AM? Although it is not impossible it is largely impractical. You see the phone rarely rings at 6AM to distract you. Employees who start at 9AM rarely need help at 6AM. Clients and suppliers do not like to schedule meetings for unimportant things at 6AM. Thus, your rested decision-making abilities can be fully deployed on your biggest limiting factors without interruption during these golden morning hours.

Utilizing the morning to your advantage becomes even more important if you are raising a family. Starting early allows me to tackle tasks before a baby cries or a child suffers a 5-alarm emergency trying to locate a missing school project. All of which, deteriorate intellectual capacity. Moreover, your family does not miss you if you work while they are sleeping. However, if you do not come home in the evening before they go to bed, you miss out on key opportunities to bond.

How do you rewire your internal clock? Like a lot of things in life, the path to progress is neither attractive nor complicated. Start waking up at the same time consistently. The worst that will happen is you will miss a night or 2 of sleep fretting about the early wakeup call. Thus, enduring a couple of days in a zombie like state. I believe an incremental change, or a weird napping schedule is largely a waste of time for most. Many people have developed the early rising ability just like people develop the ability to run marathons. Your body will adjust. Just like it does for daylight savings time or time zone changes during travel.

"A culture of discipline
is not a principle of
business, it is a principle
of greatness."
- JIM COLLINS

YOU CAN WORK 5-DAYS PER WEEK

*"CEO's work an average of 6
hours per weekend." – CNBC*

Unfortunately, we find the entrepreneurs who tell us they are not available for Saturday appointments tend to make less money. It is not unusual to be sitting with a successful business owner at 8AM on a Saturday morning. However, clients with cashflow problems rarely gravitate towards that appointment slot.

In absence of significant entrepreneurial experience and working capital, 60-80 hours per week tends to be the likely formula to build a successful business. When you start to plot this out on a calendar, you begin to find that it is impractical to fit that into a 5-day workweek.

I am a big proponent of a 6-day workweek. So long as you start early, it makes working the required hours to build a business and maintaining a family life possible. Saturdays become an incredibly useful day. Like mornings, there tends to be fewer distractions. Thus, they can be used for strategic or complex tasks. Also, clients who are unavailable Monday to Friday are often available on Saturdays.

I do caution people against a 7-day workweek. In my experience, most entrepreneurs who tell me they work 7-days per week are less productive. Rather than executing a plan that strategically devotes sufficient time to the most important tasks, they tend to just be bouncing from task to task as they come in, in a perpetual state of disorganization.

I have experimented with a seven-day workweek and have found that it does not increase productivity long term. However, it certainly has a negative impact on family life. I find my focus is sharper and I am often able to come up with better ideas if I take a full day off each week. Remember, business is not a sprint it is a marathon. Thus, your schedule must be sustainable over years, not weeks.

"Multitasking is merely the opportunity to screw up more than one thing at a time."

– GARY KELLER

YOU CAN MULTITASK

"We lose 28% of an average workday to multitasking ineffectiveness." – The One Thing

At some point we probably watched a movie that included a character portrayed as successful and hyper-productive. They were likely attached to their cell phone, had what appeared to be multiple projects on their desk, and had employees running through their door looking for immediate attention. Yet, I cringe every time I hear someone say, "I'm a great multitasker".

It is because this Hollywood caricature of a productive person is an outright lie. Business is insanely competitive. The market does not pay for subpar products and services. Your competitors are going to do everything in their power to steal your customers. Being distracted is merely an unsustainable band aid that businesses owners who fail to differentiate, delegate, and plan use. They think it is all about being first. Yes, you must be responsive. However, ultimately you only win by being better than your competitors not first. Do you think Steve Jobs was getting interrupted all day long when he was perfecting the iPhone?

Deep down we know that our intellectual capacity reduces when we are distracted. How would you feel if your uber driver was filling out paperwork after setting the cruise control on the freeway? How about your surgeon discussing marketing strategy while they have you one the table?

Your calendar can shield you from the unproductive interruption trap. Building a company is a minimum 60 hour per week task. Once you accept this reality you can schedule uninterrupted blocks of time to work on your most important initiatives. Ideally in the morning when no one is looking for you.

Do not feel guilty about shutting off your phone or email during these precious strategic time blocks. Try to hire an employee or even a call centre to shield you from interruptions as early as practical in the business. I do not mean someone who just greets the person before they pass on the message to you. I mean someone armed with scripts and a calendar, who can action tasks as they come in, and schedule them as required.

It is our employee upbringing that tells us we have to drop everything when the boss calls. The problem is that when you are a business owner, every customer becomes your boss. The seeds of greatness are within you, but they exist only within your solitaire maniacal focus. Stop trying to be a good receptionist and start trying to be the best in your industry!

"Live your passion. What does that mean, anyway? It means that when you get up for work every morning, every single morning, you are pumped because you get to talk about or work with or do the thing that interests you the most in the world. You don't live for vacations because you don't need a break from what you're doing—working, playing, and relaxing are one and the same. You don't even pay attention to how many hours you're working because to you, it's not really work. You're making money, but you'd do whatever it is you're doing for free."

– GARY VAYNERCHUK

THAT YOU CAN WORK 9 TO 5

"70% of all consumer bricks and mortar
spending takes place after 6:00pm."
– Alexander Communications

I cringe every time I hear a rookie entrepreneur say they do not work past 5. The problem is the most affluent buyers are often tied up until then. Think about it for a minute. People who become wealthy, often have a habit of not cutting out of work early. As such, entrepreneurs who refuse to work in these key buying hours significantly reduce their chance of success.

Being that I started my business career in construction, I had already come to this conclusion. Often homeowners who had money to spend on renovations were only available to meet after their workday. Thus, when I started my accounting firm, I decided to take evening appointments.

Customers will often tolerate CPA's and other professionals who restrict their availability to standard business hours. Often the entrepreneurs in these industries will use this industry norm as an excuse not to stay late. However, in working with other professional clients I have found that working in late in an industry that closes early, is a sure way to gain market share.

I know most people start a business with the vision of better work life balance. I hope I have convinced you that this should be a long-term goal and not a short-term goal. However, the question you should ask is, how these expanded operating hours will affect the long-term goal of better work life balance?

I have gotten to the point now that no matter what timeslots I open for customers, they will always fill, even at 6AM. This took a long time and a lot of hard work. That said, I still offer evening appointments and plan to do so indefinitely. I have seen how useful they are in booking facetime with other hard workers and how appreciative people are when they know you are willing to stay late for them. I have found that working longer days facilitates the ability to take more full days off. This facilitates more family vacations instead of operating in a perpetual state of semi-distraction when you get home from work in the evening.

"If you are what you
repeatedly do, then
achievement isn't an action
you take but a habit you
forge into your life."
– GARY KELLER

THAT YOU CAN'T ASSEMBLE A REPEATABLE CALENDAR

"75% of a CEO's time is scheduled in advance." – Harvard Business Review

Almost every inexperienced entrepreneur I meet thinks managing your day is an artform and everyday is the opportunity for a new masterpiece. However, this is almost always a recipe for going broke. Conversely, experienced entrepreneurs have often been working a rigid scheduled routine for years.

I just met today with someone who has been in business for 42 years. The health of his lifelong accountant is failing, and his old school paper ledger system is archaic. However, his numbers were relatively accurate, and he has effectively beaten the odds by operating a business for longer than 10 years. Drilling in further I find that he has been executing a bi-weekly accounting process for decades. Further, he has a set schedule to deal with the production side of the business and he has other dedicated times sets aside to maintain his critical equipment.

The rookie entrepreneur thinks that this regiment is either undesirable or only possible once you have been in business for years. The experienced entrepreneur knows that you only get to stay in business for years if you find a repeatable schedule that works.

The repeatable schedule forces you to think critically about the key tasks in your business and allocate a reasonable amount of time to each. Thus, ensuring that you do not neglect any key functions. Most importantly it provides perpetual guidance on which tasks are unimportant. There will always be more things requesting your attention than hours in the day and it is common for the least important things to yell the loudest.

Think about the telemarketer trying to sell you something. The difficult customer who will never be satisfied. The employee who always has an issue with the co-worker. As I write this book, I know I have not yet selected the colors for renovations at our office, the online pricing for tickets to our business bootcamp is posted incorrectly, and I am overdue with my banker to discuss refinancing options on the real-estate I own. Yet I have scheduled the time to write this book as it increases my ability to build rapport with people in other markets and continue to scale my business. Knowing that growing the business is far more economically important than the color of the new office, I stick to the schedule. After all, I have the piece of mind knowing I have time in my calendar every week to deal with these administrative issues.

Do not be overly concerned with getting your template calendar right the first time. You must try it and adjust. Once you find a calendar that you are sticking to 80% of the time, you might just have a sustainable business on your hands!

"If you live for vacations and
weekends your shit
is broken"**- GARY VAYNERCHUK**

THAT YOU GET SIGNIFICANT VACATION IN THE EARLY YEARS

*"54% of entrepreneurs will take 2 weeks
or less vacation per year." – Score.org*

We work with a lot of new business owners and our meetings with our clients are usually scheduled 30 days or more in advance. When choosing meeting dates with new business owners it is not uncommon to find that they cannot make a proposed date due to a vacation.

There are several problems with vacations during the infancy of your business. First off, the relationships with your customers are new. Thus, the chances that a customer will terminate the relationship because of any shortcoming in service while your away is increased. Secondly, you will either have employees who have not been with you that long or no employees at all. As such, it is unlikely that you will have someone on the team who can hold down the fort. Finally, vacations are expensive! When you own a business, you do not just have to deal with the cost of the vacation, you have to deal with the likely reduced revenue while you are away.

I did not take a full week vacation until around the 4-year mark of my accounting firm. I would take a few extra days here and there, but not a full week. Even then, I was likely working remotely a few hours each day. Looking back on it, I was likely too hard on myself and those around me. After all, I have found that completely disconnecting for a week tends to help me make better decisions. Still when I hear a business owner a few months in planning their 3-week European vacation, I get scared. I know that they will likely being paying for that trip on their credit card for years afterward.

I think taking more than 1 or 2 weeks per year in the first few years is a recipe for disaster. This assumes that you are working a minimum of 6 days and 60 hours per week the rest of the year. Now I do not mean 6 days a week unless it's your birthday, you have the sniffles, or if there is a holiday that week. I mean 6 days a week EVERY SINGLE week of the year except those 1 or 2 weeks.

Please do not get me wrong, I love vacations and I view entrepreneurship as gateway to realizing a goal of increased vacation time. I now schedule 10 weeks vacation every year. I have found that it adds to my life more than just coming home an hour earlier. It is during these weeks off, that our family truly does spend more time bonding and doing amazing things, rather than just going through the motions while being distracted from what happened at work earlier that day. However, if you take too much vacation early on, it is likely on borrowed money. This strain on cash flow often prevents the required investments to create a machine that is capable of functioning without you. Ultimately that self functioning business machine, is the freedom you are looking for. Not a 3-week vacation in year 1.

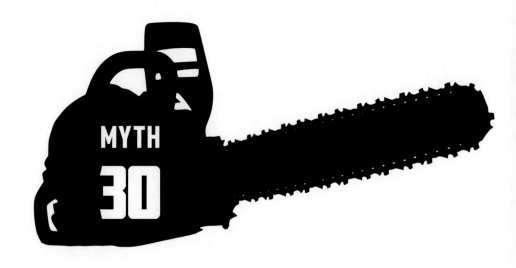

"A good leader does not get
bogged down in the minutia
of a tactical problem at
the expense of strategic
success."
– JOCKO WILLINK

THAT YOU DO NOT NEED TIME FOR SOLITARY STRATEGIC WORK

"CEO's spend 28% of their work time alone." – Harvard Business Review

Often, we hear of business owners who are putting in the hours but not getting the results. However, when you drill deeper you find that all their time is spent on location with employees, with suppliers, or with customers. Then like the hamster on the wheel, they simply run faster and faster wondering why they are not making progress.

Businesses at their core are entities that get paid to solve problems. Unfortunately, our problem-solving skills are often impaired in the presence of others. The learning and outside the box thinking required to outperform the competition is normally facilitated by solitary strategic work.

The need for solitary work often goes hand in hand with waking up early. Customers do not like meeting at 6 in the morning. Most employees will not be vying for you time at that hour. Thus, the easiest time for a business owner to isolate themselves is in those early morning hours.

It is during these solitary sessions that you can think critically about how your calendar is allocated. These are the times that you use to improve your marketing and sales scripts. These are the times that you use to write the checklists and templates required to consistently deliver your product or service at a higher level. These are the times that you increase your knowledge and skills, allowing you to deliver more impactful employee training sessions. Thus, the appointments with yourself are often the most important appointments of all!

"Tackling these tasks
in the order we receive
them is behaving as if the
squeaky wheel immediately
deserves the grease."
– GARY KELLER

THAT YOU SHOULD TACKLE TASKS IN THE ORDER THEY ARE RECEIVED

"75% of a CEO's time is scheduled in advance." – Harvard Business Review

I have heard entrepreneurs tell me that they respond to all emails, texts, and phone calls within an hour. They usually say it with a sense of pride. When they make the declaration, you can usually see the virtuous light shooting out of them as if they just irradicated hunger around the globe or negotiated world piece.

Thus, they are normally confused when I tell them they must stop doing this. Inevitably in business you must come to terms with a sobering truth. There will always be more things to be done then there are hours in the day. Time is your most valuable resource. Entrepreneurs will only be successful if they make time for what they must do by leaving things that they could do undone.

Unfortunately, rarely do the most important initiatives in your business ask for attention. We talk about it over and over. Businesses fail predominantly because of lack of customers, running out of cash, and the inability to find the right team. However, no customer will call to complain that you are not doing enough to market to other customers. Customers will never call you to remind you to review your accounting reports or call you to ask how your weekly staff meeting went. Therefore, if you tackle your day based on who calls first or what email hits your inbox first, you will fail, end of story.

Now I am not saying that you should ignore customers. However, there needs to be certain blocks of time that they can not steal from you. The most common mistake is letting customers steal time that was set aside for your marketing and sales functions, to deal with day-to-day customer issues. Thus, speeding up the doom loop of retaining only increasingly difficult customers with no way to replace them.

Then there are items that you should ignore all together. Clients will often ask how to respond to suppliers reaching out trying to sell things. Most of the time the answer is do not respond at all. Even when they are trying to sell you a better piece of software for your business or materials that are a few percentage points cheaper. If you do not have your marketing, accounting, and staff training done almost everything else can wait.

Then when it comes time to deal with customer issues. Have specific times in your calendar blocked out to deal with these issues. Make it a regular part of your week but do not let it go overtime. Then look at delegating things to increase your service level.

MYTH
32

"There is a temptation in
our networked age to think
that ideas can be developed
by email and iChat.
That's crazy."
– STEVE JOBS

TEXT & EMAIL ARE EFFICIENT FOR BACK-AND-FORTH COMMUNICATION

"It takes an average of 23 minute to reach your peak level of intellectual capacity once you are interrupted." – The One Thing

Before I switched to flat monthly fees, as a CPA, I spent the better part of decade selling my life in increments of 15 minutes. Now your risk adverse friends who work for the government will swear by getting everything in writing. However, after running a business I can tell you written communication is incredibly inefficient for any form of back-and-forth communication.

I fully realize that it is often quicker to get a response by text or email. However, providing responses quickly is always less important than finishing tasks. The chances that you will get a significant block of undivided attention from anyone on the other end of a text is slim. Also, written communication almost always involves starting and stopping tasks. Once I found out that it takes approximately 23 minutes to regain peak intellectual performance after switching tasks, I started to understand why relying on back-and-forth written communication made tasks take longer.

Before all the lawyers reading this have a heart attack, I am not suggesting that you do not put things in writing. I am merely suggesting that you attempt to limit the back-and-forth written communication leading up to the formal final written advice, contract, proposal, etc. In other words, written communication should be used to close and document the communication loop.

Often people start down the path to collaborate efficiency in a meeting and then fall off by agreeing to continue the process by email. Then the perpetual wheel of incomplete solutions begins to flow from everyone on the thread, causing you to switch attention back and forth, robbing you of your intelligence 23 minutes at a time. Alternatively, people should leave a meeting with specific homework and a specific date or time to review the completed project in person or by phone. Then once the project is done, written documentation should be used to document the completed work.

This efficiency hack will be further complicated by a younger generation who was raised on a steady diet of text and email. Often, they are afraid of the phone. However, you simply need to push the baby birds out of the nest. Although some will never progress beyond what sounds to be a nervous prank caller, others will gain confidence and potentially begin to fill the void of human connection that is often created by overreliance on text and email.

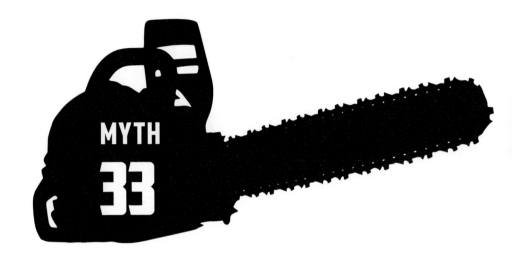

"Task switching exacts a
cost few even realize they
are paying"
– GARY KELLER

THAT YOU HAVE TO CORRESPOND BY TEXT OR EMAIL

"On average 61% of a CEO's time is spent in face-to-face interactions."
– Harvard Business Review

I am sure you have heard someone in your life before say "get everything in writing". It is usually advice given by someone who has never risked what is required to build something substantial. I am not suggesting that you can do everything by a handshake in business. There is a time and a place where written communication can reduce your risks substantially. However, there are a couple of problems with written communication.

Firstly, it is slow. Now I know you have been indoctrinated by the technology companies to think that texts, emails, and social media updates are the future of quick communication. For superficial defined issues, that may be true. However, making business decisions involves back and forth inquiry, brainstorming, understanding personalities, and talking through multiple potential outcomes. Although it is often quicker to take the next step through written communication, it's usually slower to reach a conclusion via the on again off again often distracted drip that we know as written communication. Moreover, whenever we switch from one conversation thread to another, we become less efficient and more prone to mistakes.

Business is not about working on tasks. Business is about finishing tasks. Thus, although in person meetings and phone conversations often take longer to initiate, it will often bring a task to resolution quicker than start and stop written communication.

Secondly you will not reduce your risk to zero by communicating in writing. This myth is routed in the education system that insinuates life as being a multiple-choice test with one no risk "correct" answer and other incorrect answers. This is simply not the case in the real world. In the real world it might take too long to get the answer in writing. Even if you get it in writing there may be no mechanism to hold them to account. It may be too expensive to litigate or the too difficult to tie direct damages to a specific task.

You should not be afraid to see an issue arrive in written form and instead pick up the phone or schedule a meeting to talk it through. Even if that person responds to your voicemail with more written communication, pick up the phone again and leave them another voicemail explaining to them that because this issue is important you want to take the time to have the back-and-forth discussion. Do not grind the key functions of your business to a halt or interrupt your valuable family time to engage in inefficient back and forth written communication. Sometimes these discussions are scary because they initiate conflict. However, it is my experience insisting on a discussion does not trigger unnecessary conflict it only accelerates inevitable conflict. Being that discussions are more likely than written communication to resolve conflict, insisting on discussions is the ultimate time hack.

"Motivation gets your going
and habit gets you there."
– ZIG ZIGLAR

WILLPOWER IS UNLIMITED

"It takes on average 66 days to form a
new habit." – Entrepreneur.com

I often find entrepreneurs who are overly focused on motivation. It is not unusual for an entrepreneur to spend thousands of dollars on motivational seminars and online courses only to face financial ruin a couple of months later.

Motivation is something that is useful only in moderation. I do recommend regular motivational activities. However, you must understand the addictive euphoric dopamine response that can be triggered by motivational material. This can lead to excessive time spent on motivational activities, disguised as necessary "personal development", at the expense of doing income generating activities.

I find it useful to listen to educational and/or motivational audio material first thing in the morning. I prefer audio material because it requires extraordinarily little willpower to stick a headphone in your ear and hit play, after the alarm clock goes off at 5AM. Even before your feet hit the floor. Whether the material is educational or more motivational in nature, it allows me to start the day off with a win, with little effort. This momentum can sometimes carry me throughout the day.

That said, I am not expecting to feel motivated before I act. I rely on my habits and more specifically my calendar to get me moving in the right direction. You are not going to feel motivated every morning. You are rarely going to feel motivated to do your least favourite tasks. Although we can use little tricks like audio in the morning to maximize the chances of motivation, sometimes what you need to do is going to feel awful.

Instead of endlessly searching for motivation during the inevitable lulls, you should double down on sticking to your calendar during these challenging times. As the most sustainable motivation, stems from accomplishment, and accomplishment in the business world is not possible without sustained effort over years on strategic tasks.

"If you don't plan your time
someone else will help you
waste it."
– ZIG ZIGLAR

BURNING FIRES SHOULD STEAL TIME FROM STRATEGIC INITIATIVES

"Only 25% of the average CEO's time is spent on unscheduled tasks." – Harvard Business Review

The single most important page of information we give clients throughout the year is the milestones section of the business plan. It is one page with sequential monthly strategic initiatives. It contains things your customers will likely never ask for but are the most important things to do, to move the business forward. For example, assembling a list of ideal referral partners, implementing a strategy to gather testimonials, relaunching a website, starting a recruiting strategy, implementing staff training sessions, etc.

Clients will sometimes return at the end of the year with little progress on the strategic initiatives. Often, they cite dealing with day-to-day fires as the reason they did not progress. After all, the easiest appointment to miss, is the one with yourself.

These business owners think that they will have time to step back and do these strategic initiatives once they are more established. However, I find that that this is not the case, as businesses do not become established unless they prioritize these items to begin with. I find most successful entrepreneurs simply tackled the strategic initiatives in the early morning hours before anyone was trying to reach them.

I believe the natural ego of business owners tends to inflate their opinion of their own problem-solving skills. I have had to battle with this personality trait myself. However, as you gain experience you begin to see that if you empower capable people, they make good decisions. It may not be the same decision you would make, but 80% of the time it will get the job done. Also, even if you do get involved, there tends to be a significant law of diminishing returns on the amount of time that you spend. Often providing a little coaching to a team member assigned to the task, will help them do work that saves you significant time.

Even the time that successful business owners spend on unscheduled tasks tends to be scheduled. As they often allot extra time for appointments to deal with issues in between or simply carve out a spot on the calendar to deal specifically with "burning fires".

As the team grows, you are going to want a short, daily team huddle to deal with unique issues. Not only does this allow you to avoid the "do you have a minute" interruptions throughout the day, but it allows you to teach the entire team how to deal with unique issues all at once. This avoids the inefficiencies of coaching team members one by one. Beyond that, you are likely going to want to have time set aside to work with managers or more senior staff, to work through more complex issues as they arise.

"A manager is not a person
who can do the work
better than his men; he is
a person who can get his
men to do the work better
than he can."
– ZIG ZIGLAR

THAT YOU SHOULD DO EVERYTHING YOURSELF

"54% of businesses have less than 5 employees." – Industry Canada

How many times have your heard "if you want something done right you have to do it yourself"? In many client meetings I hear some iteration of this statement. It is usually some problem where the business owner has convinced themselves that the only way to solve the problem is for them to take over a task. As if no one else on the planet could possibly possess the skills and abilities required in that moment.

One of the most amusing conversations I have with business owners is when they convince themselves that they are the only ones who can possibly answer the phones for their business. They often go as far as convincing themselves that answering the phones until retirement is going to give their business a long-term strategic advantage. I call it Chief Receptionist Officer syndrome.

When you look at the issue you find that we are taught from an early age to roll up our sleeves and pitch in to get things done when required. It is a universal truth that people willing to put in the work are more valuable than those who avoid the work being done. However, the people who can effectively delegate tasks are not the same as those avoiding work. In fact, those who can effectively delegate and lead teams are often highly paid.

To the untrained eye those who avoid work and those who delegate will appear similar. However, those who delegate usually had to exceed the work ethic of those who were simply willing to do the work at some point in their career.

Those who delegate started off doing the work themselves and honing their skills. While juggling that workload, they spent additional time writing checklists and templates of their abilities. They spent even more time recruiting people suitable to execute those checklists and templates. Then once they hired that person, they spent time training them. Initially the new hire likely slowed them down. Yet most people just see the result where the entrepreneur is eventually surrounded by a team that makes their life easier. They do not see that the successful entrepreneurs normally gained the ability to delegate tasks by exceeding the output of those who were only willing to roll up their sleeves and get the job done by themselves.

"You must fire bad
customers just as you
would fire a bad employee.
If you do not get rid of your
bad employees, the good
employees will leave. If I
do not fire bad customers,
not only will my good
customers leave but many
of my good employees will
leave as well."
– ROBERT KIYOSAKI

THAT ALL CUSTOMERS CAN BE MANAGED IN A REASONABLE AMOUNT OF TIME

"10% of customers will be difficult." – Inc Magazine

Often, I will speak with a client who has clearly just dealt with a tough customer situation. They usually have some plan to dramatically change their business and avoid this difficult situation in the future.

Then I ask the question. Have any of your other customers had a similar complaint before? Often, the busines owner will say no. Then I must let them in on the secret, no business has 100% satisfaction. The goal should be to sell something that people are happy with 9 times of 10.

Business is not about switching directions at every challenge. It is about finding a repeatable process that works 90% of the time to solve a problem. If your expectation is to find something that works 100% of the time, you will never find the repeatable process, and you will never scale.

The doom loop is spending copious amounts of time dealing with difficult customers. Some people are unrealistic. You need to replace these customers as soon as possible. Get them out of your business even if they pay you. If you do not, you will find yourself ignoring the initiatives that grow the business to deal with unrealistic customers. These customers often become more and more unrealistic, the more attention you give them.

Then you also must consider the impact these terrorist customers will have on the moral of your team. Even if you can put up with them, can you find employees who will also? Remember, without a team you have no way to service the good customers at scale.

"Life is simple, but we insist
on making it complicated"
- **CONFUCIUS**

THAT YOU SHOULD SPEND TIME TRYING TO AUTOMATE ALL REPETITIVE TASKS

"79% of business customers rate the ability to interact with someone they see as a trusted advisor who adds value to their business, rather than just a sales rep, as a critical factor when choosing a service provider." – Salesforce.com

A few years back I had a client selling security systems. He paid to develop a beautiful website with a detailed customer driven online quoting system. You would think that in our modern app driven world that this would give him advantage. However, fast forward a couple of years and that company is no more.

Conversely, I did a consult recently with a security system company that has rocketed to 7 figure revenue within the first few years. Did they have a better website or app? Quite the opposite. The owner was a former sales trainer. He was the guy in charge of rookie salespeople trying to sell door to door. Thus, when he started his company, he did just that. He hired staff and trained them to sell door to door. Now he is looking to improve his web presence and search engine optimization.

This does not just relate to sales. We helped one of our clients hire an administrator in the aesthetics field. The allure of discounted products makes the position highly desirable and generates a large volume of applicants. Knowing this we got smart, or so we thought. Normally we hire through group interviews and all applicants get templated responses. However, we do take the time to personalize each email response with the applicant's name. Given the volume expected, we decided to set up an auto response. The auto response had all the required information, but it lacked the personal touch of adding the applicants name and the given the immediate response, it would clearly be known to the recipient that this was an auto-response.

Come group interview time we were prepared for a large group of applicants but were surprised when very few applicants came. We repeated the process again the following week. Instead of increasing the rate of pay in the ad, we decided to run the same ad with the same rate of pay, and simply reverted to sending personalized templated email responses. The results were shocking. It was the largest group interview we ever hosted, and we were struggling to try and find room for the 40 or so applicants in our office.

Thus, the question you should ask yourself when it comes to automating repetitive tasks, is not whether you can automate but should you. Automated interactions are far less persuasive than a human touch. Although automation may save time, it decreases the rate of conversions. This may affect how many people buy, who wants to work for you, or even how many no-shows you have in your calendar.

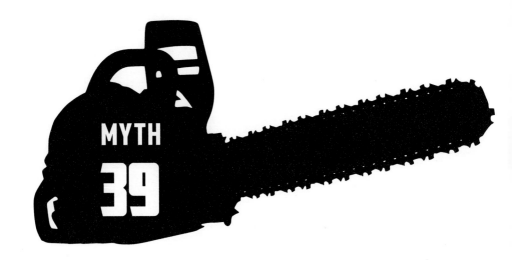

"The chief cause of failure
and unhappiness is trading
what you want most for
what you want right now."
- GARY VAYNERCHUK

THAT CUSTOMERS VALUE IMMEDIATE RESPONSIVENESS OVER EXCELLENCE OVER TIME

"35% of all appointments result in sales vs
only 18% of all walk-in traffic results in sales."
– Centre for Performance Improvement

I often find myself in a meeting and a struggling client takes a call "from an important" client. Yet the wealthier clients rarely get interrupted by their phone. I know this can become a circular argument as some will suggest that the wealthier clients can disconnect because they have people on their team to assist.

To some extent this is true, but they did not generate the money to hire the team by running around like a chicken with its head cut off answering every customer query immediately. They did it by generating value for clients. Value that customers are willing to wait for.

Do you think the highest rated business in your filed has to jump every time a customer calls to avoid running out of work tomorrow? You know the answer to this question, the truth is simply hard to face. It is ok to start there, but if you are not building systems and value from day one to get off of that hamster wheel, you won't magically figure it out once you get a couple of dollars in the bank.

It starts by gathering some social proof online that your customers can see before they reach out. It can even be as simple as recording a laser show of a voicemail. Make the voicemail make the customer feel welcome, reassure them that you value this opportunity, provides clear timelines of when you will respond.

Even businesses that chooses to differentiate themselves by speed, such as an emergency plumber, must figure out how to avoid dropping everything when the phone rings. The focus should be on writing a repeatable script to not just answer the phone but impress the customer in the way you do it. Then you focus on getting quality staff who use the script to solve the customers problems and make them feel good in the process. Now you are not just fast but good. Thus, you do not have to be the cheapest so you can afford pay someone to answer the phone for you.

I see a lot of business owners communicating back and forth multiple times per day to the same customer. Often both the customer and the business owner are sufficiently distracted to arrive at a thorough complete solution. The customer usually gets a sense of value upon the first immediate response but that feeling tends to reverse as the communication drags on. If the customer is reaching out multiple times because of a single issue, it is because your last correspondence did not solve their problem.

The business owner who focuses on being first is a commodity and that is a race to the bottom. Leave that to Walmart. Focus on being better than your competition!

"Be a maker in the
morning and a manager in
the afternoon."
– GARY KELLER

THAT OUR DECISION-MAKING ABILITY IS CONSISTENT THROUGHOUT THE DAY

"8AM to 1PM is the optimal time to make decisions." – Cognition Medical Journal

I see clients who struggle with one area of their business. Often implementing strategic marketing initiatives or completing administrative tasks. We talked about time blocking and the importance of a schedule earlier. Sometimes the client has time to complete these items on their calendar but are still not progressing.

Then you find that the client is trying to complete tedious administrative tasks after putting in a 10-hour day on the tools. You should be aware that the order and time at which you do things matter.

For example, customers tend to buy more later in the day, so focus your sales efforts there. Also, it is generally difficult to complete complex admin work later in the day or after strenuous physical work. If you think administrative work is difficult when you are tired, good luck doing high level creative or strategic work.

Allocating the correct amount of time, on it's own, does not maximize productivity. I have found that maximizing productivity is just as much about ensuring that the correct activities are assigned to the correct time of the day. I do my strategic work on my businesses first thing in the morning. This includes planning marketing initiatives, reviewing internal key performance indicators, and revising templates. I also meet with my managers before I meet with customers. This allows me to be brought up to speed before the meetings and allows me to work through complex problems prior to the fatigue that sets in closer to the end of a 13-hour day. I meet with the customers at the end of day. This gives a bit of an energy boost towards the end of the day. Also, it's far easier to explain to clients work that is already done, than complete the complex work in the first place.

Thus, when you are struggling on a task, rather than allocate more time to that task, you should experiment with doing that task at a different time in the day. Do not worry if you do not get that calendar perfect the first time. Open it up, turn the dials, and give yourself some time to experiment here.

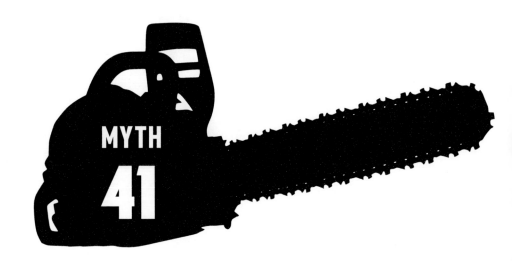

"It is unwise to pay too little.
When you pay too much, you
lose a little money, that is all.
When you pay too little, you
sometimes lose everything
because the thing you bought
was incapable of doing what it
was bought to do. The common
law of business balance
prohibits paying a little and
getting a lot"
– ZIG ZIGLAR

THAT THE CUSTOMER WILL CHOOSE THE CHEAPEST OPTION

"If presented with 3 pricing options, customers will choose the middle or top tier pricing 70% of the time." – Harvard Business Review

Most business owners struggle with pricing. I regularly hear in consults that the only way to make a sale is to be the cheapest option. I usually flip that conversation by asking them to tell me what type of car they drove to my office in. Then I point out to them that it was not a compact Nissan Versa. I point out that the Nissan Versa is one of the cheapest cars you can buy. It does not depreciate terribly. It is fuel efficient. It is relatively reliable and cheap to maintain. It is cheap to insure. Then I point out to them that it is ugly. It is too small to be comfortable and there are likely going to be cyclists that will beat you off a stop light if you buy one.

If that is not enough, I pick on their phone. It is usually a recent and pricy technological marvel. It is almost never the $50 gas station burner phone. Although the burner phone is cheaper, as Zig Ziglar said, it is unlikely to do what we want it to do.

Then once the customer is amused with my seemingly abstract examples, I go a little closer to home. I pull up the websites of their competitors who are bigger and charging more than they do.

One of the hardest things to face as a business owner is that if you can only generate revenue by being the cheapest, it is because your product or service sucks. At least, the customer thinks it does.

Sometimes your foot in the door is to be the low-cost provider or for that matter the free option. However, if you do not have a clear path with specific milestones to get out of that hell hole, your business will die. Remember Walmart is leveraging massive amounts of capital to play in that space. For the average business, owner, competing on price, will be a race to the bottom. More clearly, it will be a race to find the worst customers, using the worst products, and hiring the worst team.

You need to document social proof to increase the trust that customers have in you. You need to develop templates and checklists so you can efficiently deliver more value at market prices. Finally, you need to launch marketing that will allow you to reach your ideal and likely buyers.

"Your number-one job
is to tell your story to the
consumer wherever they
are, and preferably at the
moment they are deciding
to make a purchase."
– **GARY VAYNERCHUK**

THAT HAVING A GOOD PRODUCT OR SERVICE IS ENOUGH TO ATTRACT CUSTOMERS

"Interbrand's top 10 Global brands spend a combined 5.6 billion dollars in ads." – Mediapost.com

I meet a lot of entrepreneurs who are genuinely passionate about the product or service that they sell. Often, they are stuck in that technician role telling me about their plans to refine and re-refine their product or service in pursuit of perfection. The first problem is that perfection is something that you chase but never obtain. The second problem is, that those improvements will do little to increase demand on their own.

Interbrand's top ten include the best of the best. We are talking about Disney theme parks that are head and shoulder above their competitors. We are talking about Apple and Samsung phones which most consumers already choose. We a are talking about McDonalds where the mere glimpse of the golden arches creates instant brand recognition worldwide. Yet even these companies deploy massive amounts of advertising dollars.

Compare that to the average small business owner where the people on their street do not even know who they are. Yet, they are lost in thinking that if they improve their product or service just a little more, that the phones will start ringing off the hooks.

One of the most surprising things I learned in studying and being around successful entrepreneurs was how much time they spent pursing new business. Conversely broke business owners spend almost no time or money on generating new business.

You must remember that your job as a business owner is to wear multiple hats. In addition to the operations, you have to manage the finances, the administration, the marketing, and sales. As most entrepreneurs start a business in an industry that they use to be an employee in, what you should be doing will feel unnatural.

It will fee weird to allocate such a large percentage of your day "off the tools". It might feel normal to buy expensive tangible equipment to get better at your craft, but it will not feel normal spending for seemingly abstract marketing initiatives. Just remember the biggest single threat to a business statistically is lack of customers. Thus, you should allocate your time and your resources accordingly.

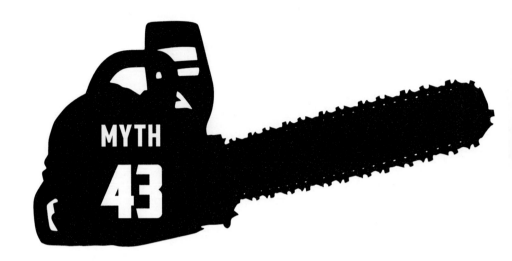

"The best place to hide a
body is page 2 of Google."

**– ANYONE WHO TALKS ABOUT
MARKETING**

THAT ANY WEBSITE WILL GENERATE LEADS

"91.5% of search engine clicks occur on the first page of search results. The rest of the pages only make up 8.5% of the clicks." – Leverage Marketing

Most business owners are obsessed at start up with launching a webpage. It said in the movie, Field of Dreams, "if you build it, they will come". However, launching a website that does not rank on Google is a lot like building a baseball stadium in the middle of nowhere and hoping for people to show up and start buying tickets. Except unlike in the movie, no one is going to show up.

The average start-up should be more concerned with starting a "Google My Business" listing or "Google map" listing and gathering 40 reviews. 40 reviews being one more than the average company that has 39 google reviews. A map listing with 40 reviews without an attached website has the potential to show up on page 1 of Google, in the map results. This ranking is dependent on the distance from which the person searching is from the business address and on the competitiveness of the keywords being searched. However, a free high ranking Google map listing with no webpage and 40 five-star reviews, is likely to generate more business than a beautiful $10,000 website buried on page 8 of the search results.

Now I am not suggesting that you should not do a website. You should have a map listing with at least 40 reviews and an effective website. The most important part of the website being the home page and specifically "above the fold" on the home page. This being the part of the page that can be seen before scrolling and most commonly as it appears on a mobile device. The reason, is that many visitors to your site will decide if they are interested, based not just without clicking on another page, but without even scrolling below the fold.

Thus, you are going to want to include a "no brainer offer" above the fold on the homepage. It needs to be more than just a free consult. For example, a discount on the first service, a free info product, or a free physical product. You also want to have 3 calls to action above the fold. For example, your phone number, email, and a "contact us" button that leads to a form. These things are necessary because the customer takes extraordinarily little time in reviewing your website to determine if they are interested in your product or service. Thus, you need to take your best shot right at the top.

Once you have this type of website and 40 reviews, you are ready to launch some ads. Search ads are a predictable way to show up on page 1 of the Google search results. Long term you are going to rank on page 1 in the organic search results below the paid ads. However, this requires time and writing copious amount of unique content about your product or service.

"Nothing happens until
someone sells something"
– PETER DRUCKER

THAT YOU CAN AVOID SALES

*"42% of failed business owners will
report lack of customers as one of
the primary issues." – Palo Alto*

Startup's often come to me with complicated models with wildly aggressive projections. I believe they can sense my apprehension when they start projecting millions in sales in their first business plan. Thus, they normally double down on how unique their idea is and how big the market is.

Then I ask the singular question, "what are your sales so far". Oddly enough the more optimistic the project, the more likely that they will tell me that the business has no sales. In fact, often they have never sold anything in their life, in any business or job.

At this point in my career, I would be far more impressed with a start-up entrepreneur who comes in with zero projections but a well thought out sales system. Customer intake script, template appointment booking email, a sales script, one sheet describing their differentiation factors compared to competitors, a closing line, and objection handling scripts. Unlike business plans with fancy modeling, the critical drivers of revenue are simply not taught in business school.

As a new entrepreneur you are likely not going to be able to afford quality salespeople. This is likely a brand-new skill that the average entrepreneur needs to learn and you should spend far more time learning about it than the time you spend laying out your new business card.

Even if you think you have some sales skills, business owners should start selling their minimal viable product as soon as possible. After all, there is no better market research than standing in front of actual paying customers. Also, those first few sales are often the life supply of cash flow that prevents breaking the bank in the early stages.

Even if a business has enough capital to hire salespeople, an owner without any sales experience is normally a disaster. After all, business is a game of influence. If not you, then who is going to convince the employees to work there in the first place. Who is going to convince the salespeople to not go rouge and do their own thing? Salespeople are notoriously difficult to manage, and this difficulty raises exponentially for the business owner who has no standardized sales systems. Moreover, if the business owner has sales experience, they can normally devise a sales system that can be deployed by less experienced and far less costly sales staff.

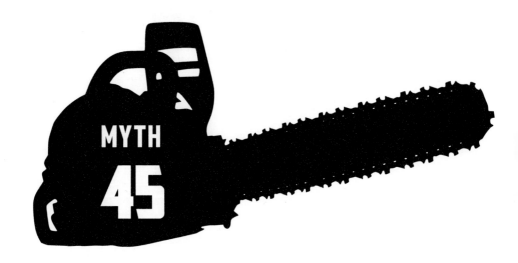

"If people like you they'll
listen to you, but if they
trust you, they'll do
business with you."
– ZIG ZIGLAR

THAT PEOPLE BUY FROM FACELESS BUSINESSES

"Brands can experience a 20-40%
increase using a celebrity endorsement."
– Harvard Business Review

I find that business owners often are not present on their own websites and if they are it is almost as if they are an afterthought. When you talk to the business owner, they usually have a misguided reasoning about building a brand. The theory being that if they focus on the brand and not themselves, then someday the business will be worth more because the owners face is not all over the website.

First off this is not a major factor in valuations. If the owner is the only one who knows how to deliver the product or service, that can be an issue. However, using the owners smiling face to gain the customers trust on the website does not tend to affect the valuation. Business valuations are heavily guided by earnings and without sales there are no earnings. Most of the time, the team page, including the bios of the people who work for the business, will be the second most viewed page after the home page. Thus, people are normally more concerned with who they are dealing with than the exact specifications of what that they are getting, as identified on the product and service pages.

Big brands know that attaching people to products moves the needle in sales. That is why Nike paid Michael Jordan to help them sell shoes and GoDaddy paid Danica Patrick to help sell websites. Both brands have far more brand awareness than the average business owner can dream of. However, despite the brand awareness, these brands know that combining people with brands generates trust and ultimately sales.

If you are the average business owner, dedicate a page on your website to the team. Put effort into making the bios unique and compelling. In fact, the team members are so important that the owner should have an abbreviated bio on the homepage. One of the best things to put below the fold on a homepage is the owner talking in their own words about what makes this business unique. Let the customer see the people behind the brand, let the customer know the stories of the people who work there, and let them hear their voices.

"People don't care how
much you know until they
know how much you care"
– ZIG ZIGLAR

THAT YOU CAN SELL A PRODUCT OR SERVICE THAT YOU ARE NOT SOLD ON

"The moral stress of deception decreases performance by 20%." - Entrepreneur.com

In doing consults, I find that a lot of business ideas are based on a perception that some industries will provide an easy path. The problem is that business success has very little to do with the idea and a lot to do with the execution of that idea. That is why I encourage people to pursue businesses in products and services that they believe solves a real problem for real people. Ideally something that you are passionate about.

I have talked about how the road to creating a successful business is usually a decade in length. The number of hours required are staggering. Regardless of how brilliant your idea is or how underserved that market is, the burden of pushing something you do not believe in will likely eventually crush you. Especially for someone who has never built a business before.

Every single day you are going to have to persuade people to buy into your idea. You must ask customers relentlessly to buy from you. This is a far easier task if you genuinely believe that if they do not buy from you that they are likely to have a negative outcome with a competitor. I believe that customers can sense it when the person selling to them does not believe in their product or service themselves.

Sometimes when launching your minimal viable product, you might know that someone in the market is selling a better mouse trap. In that case your goal is to refine your offering a little each day. However, you do not sell the product while internally telling yourself that the competitor is better. You sell it knowing that although the competitor might have a better core product, the competitor does not have you and you are the one that brings the value. At this initial stage you are the one that is dealing with issues personally to know that the customer can rely on the outcome. You are the one required to use a personal touch to make the experience just a little better. Then once you have the best core product in your niche, then you scale relying on the value your product or service has by itself.

Believing in your product or service goes beyond just ensuring you stay motivated enough to put in the work or ensuring you sell convincingly. It also helps you lead. Once you figure out marketing you will realize that your company will be limited in how fast it can grow solely by your ability to develop a team. I can not imagine leading a team without believing in your product or service. Dealing with the ups and downs of people leaving, firing, and hiring. Convincing a customer in a sales pitch is one thing but convincing a team who is around you day in and day out while not believing in the business yourself, would seem incredibly emotionally taxing. So much so, that I can not see it being worth it, regardless of the financial outcome.

"The major difference
between the big shot and
the little shot is this: the big
shot is just a little shot who
kept on shooting"
– ZIG ZIGLAR

THAT EVERYONE SHOULD SAY YES TO YOUR SALES PROPOSALS

"The average close rate across industries is 19%." - Propeller CRM

Every time I hear a client tell me that they close more than 50% of their deals I get nervous. Now the client is usually surprised by my reaction because when they quote their closing rate, they expect admiration. However, when I drill into the numbers, I usually find that they are charging less than market rates.

Someone who tells me that they close 75% of their proposals is almost always making less than an employee in their industry would make. You do not have to be a sales master to close the deal if you are working for free. The problem is that you can not scale this behaviour. There is only one of you and only so many hours in the day. Then the minute you try to hire someone at a reasonable wage to delegate your tasks to, the business becomes a money losing monster.

I tell people about the rules of 3 and explain to them that to get a customer they likely need 9 leads. For every 9 people that reach out, in most industries, I would expect that only 3 are a good enough fit to even get to the pricing stage. Some people are just tire kickers looking for a hypothetical price on the phone and they are so unlikely to proceed with the work they are not willing to invest any time beyond that call. Sometimes the customer is looking for a date that you can not accommodate. Some will be looking for something that is outside of your core product or service offering. Some will book a time for a price and then never follow through. Thus, for every 9 leads you should expect to only find 3 potential buyers.

Then you move to the pricing stage. If you price 3 potential customers, you should only expect that 1 will become a paid customer. Some will be looking for bargain basement pricing options that you should not accommodate. Some will value differentiation factors that more closely align with your competitor's offerings. Some simply cannot afford it regardless of desire. Again, some will have unrealistic time or scope requirements. Although only converting 1 paid customer from 9 leads will sound bad to unexperienced entrepreneurs, experienced entrepreneurs will view that as par for the course.

Now there are things that we can do to increase this closing rate. For example, gaining more social proof, doing a better job at targeting ideal clients in marketing initiatives, and developing better sales scripts. However, you should not engage in unscalable activity just to boost a closing rate ego score.

"'Build it and they will
come' only works in the
movies" – **SETH GODIN**

THAT YOU CAN GROW A BUSINESS BY WORD OF MOUTH ALONE

"63% of companies that grow revenues do so by growing their online advertising spend." – BDC

When I hear clients talk about spending money on advertising, it is as if growing by word of mouth is the only honorable way to grow a business. However, I liken it to buying a car and not buying any gasoline to put in it. The business is your vehicle to obtain financial freedom and advertising is the gasoline required to do so.

We already identified that the top brands in the world spend copious amounts on advertising. Despite their brands seemingly infinite reach, they have found that advertising is the path to maximizing profits. From the stat above we see that advertising is the path for small businesses as well.

Every time you hear of a business built on word of mouth alone, I encourage you to look deeper. Are they driving around town in a fleet of professionally auto wrapped vehicles? Are they telling you they do not buy ads from their booth at the local trade fair? Do they brag about their referrals from the slick professionally developed website? Do their print pieces feel like they were designed by a professional graphic designer? The hypocrisy on claims of growing businesses by word of mouth alone are usually incredibly ripe.

Businesses that do not advertise can have success. However, I find that the success is usually short lived. They usually have a large percentage of their revenue tied up in their top 3 customers. Then when one of those customers pulls the plug chaos ensues because the business does not have a predictable way to replace inevitable customer turnover.

Most assume that these long-standing customer relationships will never fail them. However, I have learned they almost always do. The only question becomes when that inevitable customer turnover will occur. Will it be next month or in 10 years? I have literally seen indestructible relationships go south because the principal customer dies. Operating your business on the expectation that a particular customer will stay forever is insane.

Moreover, the moment you lose a key customer is the worst time to start marketing. The cash flow is already sideways. Your options to generate testimonials may be compromised. Also marketing initiatives take time to start working. I genuinely believe that the absolute minimum you should be spending on online ads is $1,000 per month.

"You are the average of
the 5 people you spend the
most time with."
– JIM ROHN

THAT YOU CAN GROW YOUR BUSINESS BY NETWORKING ALONE

"Conversion rates are nearly 6x higher for online content marketing adopters than non-adopters" – Upland Software.

In talking with business owners that do not spend money on advertising, I believe it is due to fear. We talked about the employee indoctrination mindset that we are taught growing up. "A penny saved is a penny earned". By comparison business networking is generally cheaper than paid advertising. Therefore, when using the employee mindset where income earning potential is fixed, minimizing costs would appear the more prudent alternative.

However, the stats do not support this. Paid marketing not only increases revenue, but it also increases profits. Now I am not saying that you should choose paid marketing over networking. I believe there is value in both. After all, being around other entrepreneurs facilitates the courage to go against the norm and make good business decisions. Thus, if there is an opportunity to spend time with other business owners and generate new business, I say do it.

However, networking has a diminishing rate of return. You only get 168 hours in the week, so it is far more practical to double your advertising spend than double the number of hours you are spending on networking activities. Thus, at some point the revenue you can generate through networking normally plateaus.

Moreover, think of the ideal people you would like to network with anyways. Would you rather network with a bustling business owner managing a growing list of clients made possible by advertising or a small thinking entrepreneur just working their friends list on Facebook? Surely you get the point. The value of networking expends exponentially based on the advertising budget of those you are networking with.

"In God we trust, all others
must pay cash"
– AMERICAN PROVERB

THAT THE SALE IS DONE BEFORE PAYMENT IS COLLECTED

"40% of Americans would not be able to pay an unforeseen $400 expense." – CNBC

I find most entrepreneurs at some point make the mistake of counting verbal confirmations as a sale. They are probably not that surprised when I tell them that they should put written contracts in place to document the terms. However, I find that they are more surprised when they find out how little security I view from the written agreement.

To understand my position, you must understand how enforcing these debts normally transpires. First off, you should likely hire a lawyer. I tell people that you should budget at least $10,000 for this type of litigation. Sometimes you can do it for cheaper, but that is never a certainty, so $10,000 is usually my minimal consideration. As soon as you do that you are going to realize that most debts under $10,000 make no sense to litigate.

Now you can sometimes recover costs in a successful litigation, but again that is never a certainty. My experience is the costs you recover are usually less than what you actually paid. Also, the time you invest in coordinating the efforts is almost never remunerated properly. Sometimes you must make an example of someone to deter others. Other times, you may want to just report them to the credit bureau. This cheaper alternative is easier to execute. It serves as a deterrent to others and can sometimes result in eventual collection should that individual look to repair their credit in the future. However, the overriding theme is that all mechanisms to collect bad debt are slow and none fully remunerate your efforts in dealing with the situation.

What do we do about it? First off, sell products and services that work to solve the problem the consumer had in the first place. Also charge fair prices and ensure the payment terms are realistic for the customer. Use deposits or third-party financing if required. Be transparent about the price, anything that would affect the price, and any cancelation terms. Then most importantly, bill them early, bill them often, and bill them on time. Moreover, follow-up on their missed payments with the same diligence you would follow-up with a new prospective customer.

People overspend in todays society. Your customers, whether they be individuals or businesses will overspend. You need to get paid as you go. You can not extend any credit that you are not willing to write off. Remember, even if you litigate successfully, it will still be a write off in terms of your short-term cash flow. Even if you can extend the credit, consider if it is worth the risk. Whatever you do, just remember, the sale is not complete until the bill is paid.

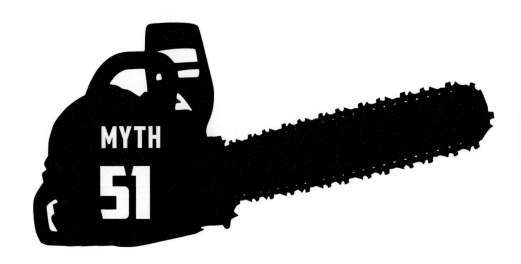

"There is no elevator to
success, you have to take
the stairs" – **ZIG ZIGLAR**

THAT YOU CAN SELL WITHOUT FOLLOW-UP

"80% of sales require 5 follow-up calls after the meeting. 44% of sales reps give up after 1 follow-up." – Bevet Group

I hear some entrepreneurs talk negatively about marketing sometimes and I can not help but think it is because they are not willing to work hard enough for a sale. Thus, the only people they have success in converting are the ones who were so desperate to solve a problem that they asked a friend, got a referral, and did not shop around. The problem is that this is a small percentage of the market. Most people are going to shop around, regardless of whether the lead comes by referral. Leads are like fish. It is your job to get them in the boat and it is going to take a while.

First off when you call a lead, do not just call them. If you have all the information, call them, leave a voicemail, send them a text, and then send them an email. Then get prepared to repeat that process every single week.

Then once you get the appointment, send them the details of the appointment by email upon booking. If you are booking more than a week out, call, leave a voicemail, text, and send an email a week before. Then do the same the day before the meeting. Sound like work yet?

Then once you get the appointment try to close them at the appointment if it is at all practical to price the product or service at the appointment. Do not waste this opportunity to close because this is the most time efficient way to generate revenue. However, if the deal does not close there immediately send the agreement for signature. Make it easy for them, send it using a digital signature program, do not make them print it and scan it. Then once that is sent call them, leave a voicemail, send them a text, and send them an email. Repeat this process every single week until you get an answer on the deal. Starting to notice a trend?

Now there is a time hack here for the follow-up. You will find a lot of sales gurus will set specific times to follow-up with specific customers. Although this increases the closing rates, it dramatically reduces your efficiency during the week as it will impose on the other critical time blocked items within your calendar. Thus, unless it is an inordinately high value deal, I would batch all the follow-up once per week. First you go through every single pending deal by call, voicemail, text, and/or email. Then you go through every lead who is not booked for an appointment by call, voicemail, text, and/or email. That is normally a time efficient solution that you put on the plate of a multi-purpose administrator or a time efficient solution for a small business owner without an admin team.

"I believe luck is
preparation meeting
opportunity. If you hadn't
been prepared when the
opportunity came along,
you wouldn't have been
lucky." – **OPRAH WINFREY**

THAT YOU CAN NOT OR SHOULD NOT SYSTEMATIZE SALES

"Continuous sales training gives 50% higher net sales per employee." – Bevet Group

Most entrepreneurs I meet, seem to think that selling is a genetic trait. One that can not be improved much less taught from scratch. Again, we see a common misconception. If you think sales can not be learned talk to someone who has done sales for 10,000 hours and someone who just started yesterday.

However, this misconception is just scratching the surface of the root issue. The issue being that most people think good sales presentations are from the hip, when in fact, the best sales presentations are perfectly planned, and repeatable. The first step being building rapport, the second step being establishing the prospects needs, the third step explaining the benefits, and the fourth step closing the deal.

Even within those steps you can systematize further. Usually, to build rapport you are going to have to tell something about yourself before the prospect will feel comfortable enough to tell you about themselves and eventually their needs. Normally you will have to tell them a story about yourself. However, once you find a story that resonates with most of the customers, keep telling it to every customer that walks in. Do not switch it up and leave it to chance.

I am talking to business owners, so I like telling them about my business journey because it's going to make them feel comfortable in telling me about their business journey. Thus, it leads naturally into establishing needs. If I was selling cars, I would talk about cars I owned. If was selling construction services, I would talk about properties I have owned and renovated. Then you should have several preplanned questions to identify their needs more specifically.

Now you are finally ready to explain the benefits that your product or service has to offer because you can now focus on the ones most important to them. You should be referencing written material in this process because we are taught to believe what we see in writing from an early age. You should be tying in stories of other customer results and include preplanned statements to eliminate objections before they are raised. For example, tell them all the things that will go wrong with a lower priced option before that objection is raised in closing.

Then you proceed to the close. Again, if you find a question that works to close keep going to it. Also arm yourself with preplanned scripts to disarm objections and reclose. Just like everything else in your business, sales can be systemized. This will allow you to be more effective and train more people to scale.

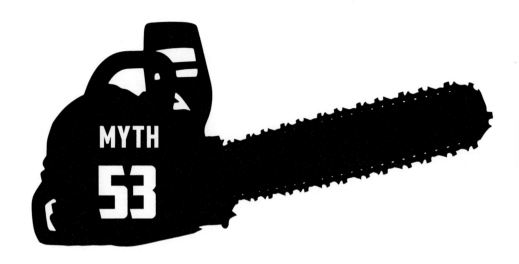

"Profitability comes from loyalty, productivity, and having a character base from which to work."
– ZIG ZIGLAR

THAT YOU NEED TO MAKE MONEY ON THE FIRST TRANSACTION.

"On average, loyal customers are worth 10x as much as their first purchase." – Marketing Tech Blog

I have worked with a couple of immigration consultants over the years. Two were of particular interest because they were opposites. One was staunchly opposed to free consults because it devalued his brand and profession. He needed his $150 for the first consult. The other would go out into field and educate hospitality chains for free, on how to hire foreign workers. Anyone want to guess which one of these providers had a 7-figure business and which one of them was struggling to get initial meetings?

It is an employee mindset to get paid for the first few hours of work. Unfortunately, we are taught from an early age to exchange time for money and there is extraordinarily little focus on providing value. Now providing value may seem like just an altruistic goal. However, I can assure you that the spreadsheets align with that goal.

Let us just start with the basic advertising costs. The average business has to spend $2.69 just to get a click on their website. What if you need 100 clicks on your website to get a lead and you need 9 leads for every paid customer. That would be $2,421 to get a customer ($2.69 x 100 x 9). Yet if you give away something for free or at a discounted rate you might be able to get one lead for every 20 clicks on the website. That would get your customer acquisition cost down to $484 ($2.69 x 20 x 9). You start to see how that $50 free item cost is a worthwhile investment. Then once the trust is built, charge a fair price.

There will always be some value hunters who will never come back after their discount. That is fine. A lot of the people who only used the free or discounted service will gladly give you a testimonial. Ultimately, you just need to get in front of enough people. Eventually you will find people who value your market differentiation factors and are willing to pay a fair price. They will often repurchase and refer like minded friends.

"It only serves to show
what sort of person a man
must be who can't even
get testimonials. No, no; if
a man brings references,
it proves nothing; but if
he can't, it proves a great
deal." **– JOSEPH PULITZER**

SOCIAL PROOF IS NOT IMPORTANT

"88% of consumers Google a business and read online reviews prior to purchasing." – Forbes

As a rookie entrepreneur selling renovation services to homeowners, I learned that they valued references. Although Google was not a thing yet, they would ask if I had any references or past customers that they could call. I soon realized that this process slowed down the sales cycle. Thus, instead of submitting a bid and references like my competitors I would bring the reference letters to the estimate. I assembled a book with the reference letters and pictures of the projects at various stages. This increased the number of jobs I could book on the spot.

Looking back on it, I wonder how many jobs I lost before I had the social proof easily accessible. How many people never got around to calling the references? How many people wanted social proof but never asked for it? They likely made up another excuse like time or cost to avoid the more difficult conversation, which was that they were not sure I could do what I was promising to do.

Fast forward a couple of decades and the psychology of people has not changed, just the medium has. People want to see social proof online. Given that most people research companies on Google prior to purchasing, you are best served by putting the social proof in the location they are doing their research. I.e. Google reviews.

This social proof will drastically affect the number of people who reach out and the rate that they close. It will also reduce their price sensitivity. People do not expect those who are highly rated to be the cheapest. Also, even after the sale there are times where you will have to ask a customer to believe in you because something does not go as planned. They are more apt to give you that trust if you have social proof thus maximizing the chance that the relationship stays intact.

This concept of social proof is difficult for entrepreneurs to wrap their heads around at times. Part of it is because entrepreneurs are more contrarian in nature. Thus, I believe they are less likely to be swayed by the herd than most. However, just think of the last time you saw a long line at a restaurant. People follow other people because it is a deep-rooted survival mechanism. Use it to your advantage!

"If you're not producing
content, you don't exist."
– GARY VAYNERCHUK

THAT MARKETING SHOULD ONLY TAKE UP A SMALL PERCENTAGE OF YOUR TIME

"The average small business owner spends 20 hours per week on marketing." – Constant Contact

When I hear how struggling entrepreneurs are spending their time or look at their calendars, the amount of time they are spending on marketing is usually inadequate. Most of the time they are struggling with cash flow which usually traces back to lack of potential customers and marketing. Yet the natural reaction for that entrepreneur will be to spend hours on hold with the phone company to reduce their phone bill by $10 per month instead of addressing the root cause.

Yet when I watch successful entrepreneurs operate, I see them spending a disproportionate amount of their time on marketing. It was almost as if running the business was an afterthought to marketing the business and finding new customers. I remember thinking that the quality must suffer. Then I saw how various time hacks made ensuring quality still possible.

A regimented calendar made sure every aspect of the business was addressed and no one thing stole too much time. They systemized routine tasks to maximize time spent on high value tasks. They had safeguards in place that people could not interrupt the calendar. They communicated efficiently through phone or in person meetings rather than endless text-based drips. They implemented efficient ways to recruit and train staff.

Then the time gained through efficiencies was reinvested in marketing and business growth initiatives. Yet so many business owners think that they can spend a few hours shopping for a marketing company, write a cheque and put this task on auto pilot.

When it comes to marketing you need to role up your sleeves and get your hands dirty. Now I am not saying you should not hire a marketing company. In fact, most business owners will hit a ceiling unless they do. However, a weekly meeting with that marketing company should be standard. Also, you should have additional time blocked out in your calendar to implement outbound marketing strategies, create content, review stats, and co-ordinate efforts with your internal team.

"You don't have to be great
to start, but you have to
start to be great."
– ZIG ZIGLAR

THAT YOU SHOULD NOT MONETIZE YOUR MINIMAL VIABLE PRODUCT OR SERVICE

"In 2007 Airbnb started with one apartment listed and the capacity for 3 guests, each paying $80 for the weekend." – Business Insider

Too many entrepreneurs come into my office with a business idea that just needs a six-figure investment or loan to get off the ground. Sometimes it is not money but that the product is so special that it will require months of product development before having a minimal viable product that people are willing to pay for. In the meantime, they have a myriad of excuses of why they can not generate any money in revenue in the months leading up to this cash injection.

First off, the odds of building a million-dollar business are only 1 in 5,000. I cannot even begin to calculate how much bleaker those odds get if the entrepreneur refuses to start until funding or a perfect product is in place.

Let us think about it from a bank's perspective or the perspective of an investor. Would you be more likely to believe someone who is selling something but could leverage money to sell more or would you trust someone with a fancier pitch deck who has sold nothing? Selling your minimal viable product is not wasting time that you could be using to seek out the funding, it is gathering the proof that someone should fund you in the first place.

Even if you are in the product development phase, there is no better market research than feedback from paying customers. After all, you are not developing a product or service for yourself. You are developing a product or service that will solve other people's problems in exchange for money.

Also spending all your time gathering funding builds bad habits. In business you must learn to wear multiple hats. You have to market, sell, produce, recruit, train, administrate, and develop a product. If you start your business prior to developing the habits that allow you to execute these multiple functions simultaneously, any sudden funding will likely just magnify the same mistakes you could have made with less money on the line. It is for this reason that so many high-net-worth people, even lottery winners, burn through cash, when they get into businesses that they have no track record in.

If you want to start a business, I recommend finding something you can sell in the first 30 days. Even something that only loosely resembles the goal product or service offering. Focus on paying the bills with this minimal viable product and devote a sustainable amount of time to product development and raising funding.

"Content Marketing Is a
Long-Term Commitment,
Not A Campaign"
– JOHN HALL

THAT YOU CAN STOP AND START MARKETING INITIATIVES

"It takes 6-9 months to start seeing results from content marketing." – Neil Patel

I find advertising is the last thing on an entrepreneur's mind when they are busy with customers. It is something they think they will get around to when they are not so busy. There are significant issues with this strategy.

First off marketing takes a while to pay off. It is usually months before you come up with the strategy, develop the content, launch the content, collect the leads, make the sale, and collect the revenue. Thus, if you wait until you need customers to start, you will likely experience a prolonged revenue reduction before the marketing starts to pay off.

In the meantime, your fixed operating costs like wages, rent, and other overhead expenses continue each month. Thus, you may not have the cash flow to execute the plan once the need becomes obvious.

Let us assume that you have a cost-effective marketing initiative that resonates with the customers. Then you turn that marketing initiative off because you get busy. Meanwhile your competitor notices the effective strategy and they copy it. Now they are distributing your message. They are making videos, writing web content, and running ads. You are going to realize that when you decide to switch back on, that the amount of time, content, and ad spend is going to dramatically increase to achieve the same results as before.

There may be times you will adjust content output and ad spend. This is not the issue, in fact, this type of testing helps you understand what is driving the ball down the field. So long as you do not make too many changes at once or adjust too frequently. However, turning the taps off completely, is a completely different animal.

You need to commit to a message to distribute to customers, commit to a distribution strategy, and do not stop advertising. You may replace initiatives over time after careful tinkering and measurement. Just do not stop.

"It always seems
impossible until it's done".
– WALT DISNEY

THAT YOU CAN AFFORD TO SPEND TIME ON QUOTING SMALL PROJECTS

"Pointless meetings will cost U.S. companies $399 billion per year." – Inc.com

One of my favourite reports to run for customers in QuickBooks is a report that shows a summary of sales by customer over the last 12 months, from largest to smallest. Then I ask business owners to consider how much time they spend on the bottom 80% of the customer list that likely only accounted for 20% of the revenue.

They usually understand the issue as soon as they see this report. However, the question is what can be done about it. Normally the answer is delegation, and that process needs to start when the client is onboarded.

In quote-based businesses there is a certain size of project, whereby if you book an appointment to provide that quote you will lose money on small projects. Let me explain. Let us say you are an electrician, and you have a $100 hourly rate and a 3-hour minimum or a $300 minimum project size. Let us say you have a 50% profit margin on your labour charge after wages, travel, shop supplies, and other overhead. Thus, you make $150 gross margin on the minimum size project. However, if you send an estimator out, after an hour of travel and an hour to do the estimate, your cost to provide the estimate is $100. Then you must consider that you normally must do 3 estimates to get one job. Therefore, that job that you make $150 on costs you $300 to estimate.

Most business owners miss this because they start out doing the pricing themselves and never consider the fair market value of their own time. It is not unusual to start out this way as it is difficult to get anyone to buy from you initially without enough social proof. However, you must transition away from spending significant amounts on quoting small projects as you scale.

Estimating is not an exact science. There is no magical procedure that guarantees you will price correctly. All you can hope to do is to allocate your time to avoid catastrophic mistakes. This usually involves pricing leads in 3 different ways.

If someone calls with a project that will take less than a day you should simply develop a script to quote your hourly rate over the phone to give the caller a reasonable range, with the goal of booking a paid service appointment. Then projects more than a day but less than $10,000 should normally be bid on the spot. With transparent and reasonable provisions for contingencies and cost overruns, with the goal of booking the job at the estimate. Then for projects more than $10,000, you should take the time to gather the scope of the project in the initial appointment and then at the conclusion of the initial appointment book a time for a follow-up appointment to provide a price. If the customer is unwilling to schedule this follow up meeting, the investment in time to provide this type of comprehensive quote, is likely not worth it.

"The quality of business communications has become poorer in recent years as people avoid phone calls and face-to-face meetings, I can only assume, in some misguided quest for efficiency."

– RICHARD BRANSON

THAT EMAILED PROPOSALS ARE AS EFFECTIVE AS IN PERSON PROPOSALS.

"87% of executives prefer face to face meetings." – Forbes

Entrepreneurs often tell me that they are emailing estimates and proposals, but they are not selling anything. Despite advancements in communications the psychology of influencing human beings is ancient. The famous Milgram experiment conducted in the 1960's showed how obedient people were to people in perceived authority roles. It also showed that obedience is higher when the authority is sitting next to you as opposed to on the phone. The takeaway for business owners, is to establish yourself as the authority and sell face to face wherever practical.

Yet here we are thinking that millions of years of evolution has been changed by the invention of email. Now it is not that emailed proposals never convert to sales, it is just that it should not be your first option. The first option should be in person, the second option should be by phone, and the fallback should be email.

Entrepreneurs always should consider the most efficient use of their time. I would suggest that selling by email is rarely a good use of time. We talked in the previous chapter that projects of a certain size can simply be sold on the initial phone call and middle of the road projects should be sold at the initial meeting to save money on quoting costs. However, quoting middle of the road projects on the spot also has the advantage of maximizing influence by selling in person.

Then we get into the higher value projects. These are more complex projects that require some contemplation prior to giving a price. With the level of contemplation required making it is impractical to quote on the spot. Generally, more than $10,000.

The temptation is to email these estimates. However, this makes little sense as these high value projects are the most important potential projects. The potential for spending excessive time to prepare an emailed quote that no one ever looks at seriously is high. Further, the chance for misinterpretation on more complex proposals rises without the opportunity to review and discuss.

Thus, I would suggest for all complex quotes to schedule a follow-up meeting before you leave the initial meeting. If the prospect refuses the meeting to present the estimate, politely insist on the basis that it would be irresponsible to evaluate the estimate without the opportunity to discuss and ensure everyone is on the same page. If they still decline, you likely have your answer on whether they were seriously considering purchasing from you in the first place. This way, you have not wasted any of your precious hours.

"One customer, well taken
care of, could be more
valuable than $10,000
worth of advertising."
– JIM ROHN

THAT YOU CAN SCALE WITHOUT REFERRALS OR REPEAT CUSTOMERS.

"Word of mouth is the primary factor behind 20% to 50% of all purchasing decisions." – McKinsey

It can be difficult to see the value from referrals and repeat customers when starting a business. Many businesses have exceptionally long sales cycles. For example, it can be years before someone buys another new car, new house, or does another major renovation. Thus, in the first few years where business owners are scrapping for immediate precious cashflow, they lose sight of how valuable referrals and repeat customers are long term.

I do not see entrepreneurs ignoring quality standards often, at least the ones who are consciences enough to reach out to a firm like ours in the first place. It is more that they do not take deliberate steps to maximize the long-term cash flow from their clients after the initial purchase.

If you sold anything that requires annual maintenance or checkups, those annual appointments should be scheduled one year out at the conclusion of service. People might be surprised at the first attempt to schedule something so far in advance. However, careful scripting will allow you to explain the benefit of the annual appointments and reassure them that they will have the opportunity to reschedule upon a courtesy reminder well in advance.

If you are selling something with a high value and a long-term warranty. Do not wait for them to call only if something goes wrong. Schedule an in person annual warranty check up. After doing an inspection to ensure nothing went wrong, is a great time to solicit new business or referrals.

If you are selling something with a lower value, it might be more efficient to simply call your prior clients once per year. Even happy customers lead busy lives and you simply will not be top of mind for repurchase or referral opportunities unless you take active steps to do so. At least send people a Christmas card.

The dividends from this can be significant. Even with home sales. The average person moves once every 5 years. Thus, if you are nurturing all of you clients towards repeat purchases and referrals, the revenue from this residual effect in year 5 could be more significant than all revenue combined in year 1.

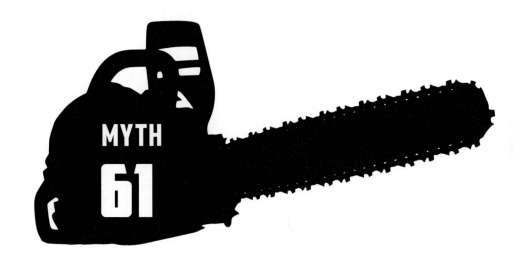

"Accounting is the language
of business."
–WARREN BUFFET

THAT MORE REVENUE WILL FIX A BROKEN BUSINESS MODEL

*"29% of failed business owners will list
running out of cash as one of the primary
reasons for failure." – Palo Alto*

Although failing to attract customers is the most common reason for business failure, sometimes I see business owners who have unprofitable relationships with existing customers. It is not unusual to see a seven-figure business come in for a consult with a cash crunch. Usually, one of the recommendations is to fire a significant portion of the staff.

When you make this recommendation, you can tell that they normally sensed as much on their own. However, it is the next piece of advice that is more shocking. That is when we tell them to fire a significant portion of their clients. This one is more counter intuitive as business owners are all about growth. However, if you have hundreds of thousand or millions in revenue and you are still not profitable you normally have unsustainable terms with clients.

We certainly do suggest adjusting the pricing prior to firing the clients. However, when the pricing levels get that far off, the drastic changes required will almost certainly result in the loss of some customers. Thus, this is usually one of the hardest pieces of advice to follow.

Generally, you want to have gross profits after covering the labour, subcontracts, and materials directly attributable to a transaction of at least 33% unless we are talking about larger projects where you are making more than $10,000 per transaction. After all, once the direct costs are covered, you still have to cover administrative staff, rent, and other overhead expenditures while still trying to maintain a healthy bottom line.

This 33% gross margin is counter intuitive for many new entrepreneurs as many entrepreneurs previously worked for bigger companies prior to breaking out on their own. Often these bigger companies could be widely profitable with gross margins of 10% or less. However, their prior employers were likely focused on 6 figure projects or higher, where the gross profit on every project was far in excess of $10,000 per project.

Once you have your margins squared away sometimes business owners must consider the cost of the administrative labor and rent for their business. These are normally the 2 most significant costs outside of the direct costs. Administrative labour can usually be changed on the fly but often it is difficult to course correct if the space you are occupying is simply too expensive.

All in all, until you have a handle on the numbers, it is sometimes impractical to sell your way out of trouble. Thus, no know your numbers and make reviewing them part of your regular schedule.

"Everyone has a plan until they get punched in the mouth." – **MIKE TYSON**

THAT YOU WILL OPERATE AT 100 CAPACITY

"Most businesses take 2-3 years to make a profit." – Freshbooks.com

Clients who come to the office for an initial consult with more detailed projections normally have overly optimistic projections. I did a consult with a restaurant who had attempted to make projections for every item on the menu. Then they project that the restaurant would be operating at capacity from day 1.

This is exactly how small businesses run out of cash. They take on costs that appear reasonable only if their unreasonable revenue projections come true.

First off, I explain to people that the planning for "every item on the menu", that they teach in business school, is useless for small businesses. If you are A&W and you sell millions of order of onion rings, you can take the time to figure out how much grease goes in the onion ring frier versus the French fry frier. However, for the average small restaurant starting out, you do not have enough data points to accurately project at this granular level. What you need to know is the average dollar value of each order and the average food cost of each order.

This is not unique to restaurants. The average electrician will not be able to accurately project the exact product split between quick service calls, panel change-outs, and lighting upgrades. The average dentist will not be able to accurately project the exact split between cleanings, root canals, and implants. Over time you can drill into these numbers. However, in the early years you will not have enough data points for this exercise to be anything more than voodoo math.

Then we must consider a reasonable rate that you will utilize that capacity in the real world. Let us say you have a 60-seat restaurant, and you can seat people every 2 hours. If you are open 10 hours per day, then you have a theoretical capacity of 300 people per day (60x10/2). Some businesses will struggle to get to 50% of theoretical capacity and some will get to 99%. However, the real-world capacity is never 100%. A restaurant will experience everything from no-shows, to dealing with awkward sized parties, to the occasional mechanical failure. Thus, I suggested for this restaurant a real-world capacity of 240 people per day (48x10/2).

Then you must consider how long it takes for marketing initiatives to pay off and attract repeat customers. I would suggest that most businesses should plan for it to take at least 24 months to hit their real-world capacity. Thus, this restaurant should expect to average 10 customers per day in month one, 20 customers per day in month two, until they hist 240 customers per day in month twenty-four. Should you aim for quicker? Absolutely! However, you should have enough cash to see this growth pattern through before starting.

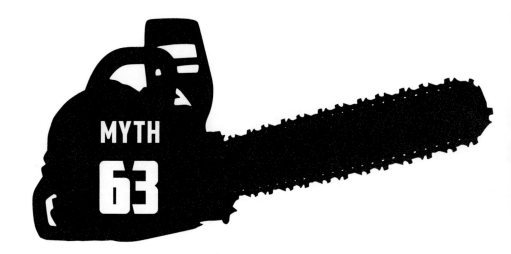

"If you cannot save money
than the seeds of greatness
are not within you."
– CLEMENT STONE

THAT YOU CAN IMMEDIATELY INCREASE PERSONAL INCOME WHEN REVENUE INCREASES

"The average gross profit margin in construction is 22% and 36% in medical." – Readyratios.com

I always start the planning process for entrepreneurs with a financial plan. Most would expect a business plan. However, I tell people unlike with big companies where you can raise capital and borrow at will, the owners' personal circumstances are directly tied to the options available for the business. There is simply no point in assembling a business plan for a small business owner and then realizing that if they wait that long to pay themselves, the bank will foreclose on their house.

Too many business owners start off paying themselves based on a percentage of revenue that is unsustainable. Then they end up missing payroll, getting behind with suppliers, or getting behind with taxes. We do a financial plan and establish a set sustainable draw each month. Knowing that the savings from a good month will be available in a slow month.

Still, I think most people vastly underestimate how much revenue you must generate to get an additional $1,000 in personal after-tax income. Let us say that you have business with a healthy gross profit margin of 35%. That means after you pay the wages or subcontracts directly involved in providing the good or service, you have 35% left over. Then let us say that you must pay taxes at a rate of 35% on any income. That means if you generate revenue of $4,400, you will have to pay direct costs of $2,860, leaving $1,540 ($4,400x35%). Then out of that $1,540 you must pay $539 in tax ($1,540x35%). Thus, leaving you with $1,001 ($1,540-$539). That means if you have healthy margins, you must generate an additional $4,400 per month to pay yourself another $1,000 per month!

Therefore, having a good handle on your personal expenditures and reducing them during start up is often a necessary trade off to start a business. You go into business because you do not want to have to worry about money and have financial freedom. However, you might not ever get there if you do not make personal sacrifices. You would be shocked to see how many business owners have $1,000 per month payments on a fancy car but can "not afford" to launch the $1,000 per month in adds that will change their lives forever. It is heartbreaking to see.

"Somehow over the years
people have gotten the
impression that Wal-Mart was...
just this great idea that turned
into an overnight success.
But...it was an outgrowth of
everything we'd been doing
since 1945. And like most
overnight successes, it was
about twenty years in the
making."
– JIM COLLINS

THAT NEW PRODUCT OR SERVICE OFFERINGS MUST BE PERFECT BEFORE YOU START SELLING

"Repeat customers spend 33 percent more than new customers." – Smallbiztrends.com

It is not unusual to look at the financial statements for an established entrepreneur and find that they have plateaued at a certain revenue level. The normal reaction is how to do we get more customers. However, do you always need more customers to sell more?

Often the answer is not to find more customers but to solve more of problems for your existing customers and in turn sell them more products or services. Normally when I see the financial statement of businesses that have plateaued, you find that their product and service offerings have also plateaued.

What you must do is look at all the things that customers who purchase your product or service purchase within a year of purchase. After all, one of the biggest barriers to selling is establishing trust. Once they have purchased from you, they would rather purchase from you again, rather than someone else. Think of the dentist selling cosmetic dental implants. That is a scary procedure for the average person to wrap their head around. They would rather purchase it from the dentist and team that just did their cleaning than someone new.

Then look at additional things that they should purchase to make the thing that they purchased originally work better or get more enjoyment out if it. I worked with a garage door repair company. He found a new product that acts as a bug screen, so people can enjoy the indoor-outdoor feel of spending time in their garage in true redneck comfort. However, I say why stop there? Let us make sure the inside of the garage is insulated, drywalled and fire taped. Then we can get the inside of the garage finish taped and painted. Then we can get some epoxy coating on the floor or even some garage floor tiles. How about a heater to make sure it is warm in the winter? Remember this is the same person who called just because their garage door wouldn't open.

When you roll this stuff out for the first time it is not going to be easy. You will not be as good at it as you are at your core services. Just realize that these things will take extra time and cost more money the first few times. There is no amount of research or product development that will eliminate that completely. The key is not more research. The key is starting.

"There's only 3 ways a
smart person can go
broke: liquor, ladies, and
leverage." **– WARREN BUFFET**

THAT IT IS OK NOT TO PAY PEOPLE

*"10% of all invoices are either
late or never paid." – Sage*

I often see business owners who are late on their payments trying to convince themselves that it is ok. That it is just one payment. That the bank, or supplier, or employee only had to wait a few extra days.

Now I am not talking about a missed payment or an administrative error. I am talking about knowing you should pay someone and intentionally delaying payment beyond the agreed terms or forgoing payment to them entirely. This is a slippery slope where a dangerous mindset takes hold. Once the business owner becomes comfortable, then it is not just one payment but multiple payments. Then it is not just a few days, but a few months.

Then the doom loop starts. Normally the business owner will convince themselves that it is just a timing issue. Thus, they start transferring money from one account to another day by day. As if making more frequent payments will somehow makeup for the fact that there is not enough money coming in to meet the obligations. Then they become comfortable. Suddenly it is ok to go on a vacation or buy a nice car even though you are overdue with some accounts. Then the first lawsuit arrives. Then another. Then the first key employee quits. Then another and this one takes a big client with them.

How do you avoid the cycle? Well one of the first rules is do not work for people who do not pay you in a timely manner. Often the business owner will convince themselves that not paying someone is ok because they did not get paid in time. However, that supplier or employee did not sign up to be your bank. Only extend payment terms that you as the business owner can cover.

Ultimately until you have profits that you can reinvest you have to invest time. Whoever came up with the slogan, "pay yourself first", is a low character person who you do not want as a customer. If you owe people money, you can not be working 40 hours per week and taking weekends off.

I am not saying that you should avoid leverage. Look at all the top companies, they have debt on their balance sheet. Setup 30, 60, or 90-day payment terms with your suppliers. Finance assets when you buy them to preserve working capital. Setup lines of credit with attractive rates. However, live by the payment terms that you agree to. Do not move the goalposts on people. In the end, business is largely a way to motivate yourself to do what needs to be done rather than what is easy to do. If you continually let other down, you will end up letting yourself down in the end.

"The word accounting
comes from the word
accountability. If you are
going to be rich, you need
to be accountable for
your money."
– ROBERT KIYOSAKI

THAT YOU CAN OPERATE A BUSINESS WITHOUT REVIEWING YOUR NUMBERS

"40% of entrepreneurs say bookkeeping and taxes are the worst part of owning a small business." – National Small Business Association

One of my favourite questions to ask business owners is, on a scale from 1 to 10 how well do you know how much money you made last month? If I hear a number less than 7 it is time for immediate action. This is easy to ignore because accounting is generally not people's favourite thing to do.

When clients are making a business decision, I generally start the meeting by reviewing the most up to date financial reports available. It is funny because sometimes you can sense a client's impatience with the process because they are ready to explain a game plan to me and well thought out reasoning that they have likely been thinking about for a while. However, experience has taught me that my opinion will be drastically affected by the current financial performance. As it is impossible to make sound business decisions without a grasp on the overall financial picture. I mean we might want to buy a fancy new piece of equipment to increase productivity long term, but we must know if we can make the payments in the short term. The most interesting thing that I have found is how often the client will agree with my opinion if we look at the financial reports first.

Now the key here is to implement an accounting protocol that is appropriate for the size of the entity. After all, we want good data that allows us to make decisions. We are not after perfect data, that is so time consuming to assemble, that it steals time from revenue generating activities.

Solopreneurs generally need to get one bank account and one credit card for the business. Then deposit all the business income to this bank account. Also pay for all the business expenses from the business bank account or designated business credit card. Most importantly, they should avoid comingling other personal income and expenses in these business accounts. Then once per month, print out the statements, go through each line item, and write notes on all the line items so you remain clear on exactly what transpired.

Once you are big enough to hire staff outside of immediate family members, have a bookkeeper reconcile the accounts before running payroll every week or 2 weeks in a double entry accounting program like QuickBooks Online. Then have the bookkeeper provide income statement and balance sheet reports for you to review. Then once you are big enough to hire 5 or more full-time employees or have more than one million in annual sales, have a CPA review these numbers with you once per month. Do not over complicate this. Do not try to become a CPA in your spare time.

MYTH
67

"Success is walking from
failure to failure with no
loss of enthusiasm."
– WINSTON CHURCHILL

THAT PEOPLE WILL ALWAYS PAY YOU

"On average, companies' write-off 4% of accounts receivable as bad debt. For a 10-million-dollar company, that means they are writing off $400,000 each year." – Anytimecollect.com

We discussed earlier how the sale is never complete until you get paid. Some of the risk mitigation tactics we discussed were getting signed contracts and billing more frequently. Clients will often nod and agree when I go through these things. However, the difficult thing to accept is that no matter the policies you adopt, you will have to deal with bad debts. Even in a retail situation, you will have theft and dine and dash customers. Writing off bad debts is a part of life.

Everyone thinks their customers are better and it will never happen to them. Somewhere there is a carpet cleaning contractor who is still waiting for Lehman brothers to pay their bill. Do you think one year before Lehman brothers collapsed that their carpet cleaning contractor thought that they would default on their small bill?

This is one of the reasons why staying small is not a good option. If you are dealing with a small number of customers, that loss is both inevitable and catastrophic. Having one customer is like riding a unicycle through traffic. Eventually you are going to get hit. You need to grow your business, so it is like driving a tank through traffic.

Even if you have enough customers you must have enough margin so that one loss is easy to absorb. If you only make a 10% margin you must sell to 10 other customers to make up for the one who did not pay you. However, if you have a 33% margin you only have to sell to 3 other customers.

Once you have the financial affairs straightened away you must consider the emotional toll that this will take. I have seen people get stiffed by a single customer and struggle for months to get back to their old revenue numbers. Structurally, nothing has changed in their business, other than the business owner devoting too much time to this issue. Just because one person does not pay, does not mean that you should pursue the next 100 good customers with any less urgency.

"One thing VCs never talk
about is how screwed
founders get."
– MARK SUSTER

THAT YOU CAN RELY ON RAISING VENTURE CAPITAL

"95% of companies backed by venture
capital are not profitable." – Tech Crunch

I run into new entrepreneurs all the time that think they are just one investor away from becoming the next Mark Zuckerberg. Although these venture capital success cases are well publicised, statistically speaking, they are an unlikely path to success.

First off it is a highly competitive environment to get money from an investor. No one ever talks about the roadkill that never gets their seed funding. Also, the time required to find funding is immense. Remember business is a competitive environment. There is always a competitor out there, trying to perfect their product or service to be better than yours. The more time you spend on raising capital, the more time your competitors have to build a better mousetrap than you.

Let us say you find the money. The smart money knows that sprinkling cash on an idea does not mean that the business is more likely to be successful. Remember 96% of all business fail and 95% of all venture capital backed companies will never be profitable. Venture capital just provides the ability for a small number of companies to scale quickly.

Venture capitalists are generally making a calculated investment on 20 different ideas or more, hoping that one or two return enough to cover the losses in the others and provide a rate of return. Knowing that, the payout and control given to the founder is normally adjusted down accordingly.

Ultimately high-risk high-reward short term strategies are normally mandated by investors instead of other strategies that might have a higher probability of success long term for the founder.

Some businesses should still try to raise venture capital. However, I suggest that no more than 1 day per week be devoted to this activity. Also, there should be a clear bootstrap strategy being executed simultaneously to deal with the likely scenario that an acceptable investment offer will never be found. If you have a business that depends on an investment, you have a fantasy not a business.

"A bank is a place where
they lend you an umbrella
in fair weather and ask for
it back when it begins to
rain." **– ROBERT FROST**

THAT A BANK LOAN
IS A CERTAINTY

*"Only 39% of businesses seeking a
bank loan are successful." – Forbes*

"Can you help me get a bank loan?". This is a common first question I get asked. Unfortunately, the answer is normally, "maybe".

When people hear this, they sometimes think that this means that you do not know what you are talking about. However, I would suggest that anyone who gives a definitive answer on the topic is less likely to know what they are talking about.

To understand why, you must understand what is happening behind the scenes at the bank. First off, the banker you are talking to is not the one who makes the decision. The banker gathers the information, formats the application to conform with the institution's standards, and submits the information to the underwriting department. That underwriting department who you do not get access to and is often in another city, reviews the application. This person who you have no influence over generally says yes or no. Meanwhile the underwriter is getting instructions from management on what types of loans to approve or not to approve. These instructions change as interest rates changes, as the economy changes, and even based on how the banks other customers are performing at that time. Thus, applying for a bank loan is like shooting at a moving target in a dark room. That is why the answer is maybe.

There are ways to maximize the chances of obtaining a loan. However, most of them are not the quick fix that entrepreneurs are looking for. The most important thing is generally to have annual CPA prepared financial statements showing increasing revenues and increasing profitability from one year to the next.

You see how start-ups have trouble getting loans. They have no history, never mind two years' worth. Some things are easier to finance than others. Generally, banks would prefer to lend for hard assets such as real-estate, leasehold improvements, and equipment. It is generally more difficult to get loans for inventory, marketing, and working capital.

No loan is a certainty until it funds. Thus, there is no point starting a business unless you have a viable bootstrap strategy. In other words, you need a game plan of how you can move forward without a loan.

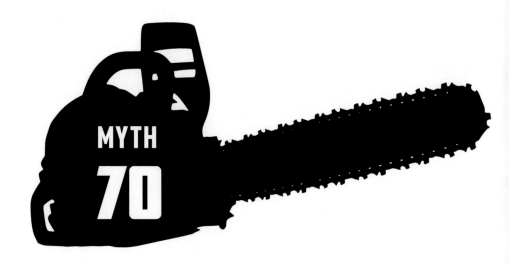

MYTH
70

"The largest locomotive in
the world can be held in its
tracks while standing still
simply by placing a single
one-inch block of wood in
front of each of the eight
drive wheels. The same
locomotive moving at 100
miles per hour can crash
through a wall of steel-
reinforced concrete five feet
thick." – **ZIG ZIGLAR**

THAT YOUR BUSINESS IDEA CAN NOT BE BOOTSTRAPPED

*"To support the start-up phase,
80% of businesses use personal
savings." – Industry Canada.*

A lot of business owners think that their business idea is dead if it does not get investor or bank financing. I disagree. I just think it means it will not be easy. As the old saying goes, "if it was easy everybody would do it".

Let us take a chef who wants to build out a million-dollar steak house with fine finishing's and fancy ovens. When they think their dream is dead when they do not get an investor or a bank loan, I walk them down the path.

Step one we start catering events using the kitchen in their house. Step 2 we take the profits and buy a food truck. Step 3 we take those profits and buyout a cheap restaurant that is going out of business. It will not be exactly what they want, but they can get it for pennies on the dollar. Step 4 you take all those profits and build out the restaurant of your dreams.

Then they ask me how long that will take. I tell them they should be prepared to spend a decade of their life pursuing this goal. Then you start to see who is serious.

Now obviously we will look for ways to accelerate this process along the way. However, the business owner who is prepared to start regardless of the existence of a shortcut at the beginning, is the one who arrives at the destination. In my experience, the person who will only start the journey if they get an initial cash injection, is the same person who finds a reason to give up later, when things inevitably get hard.

Having to be resourceful at the beginning can be helpful. It prevents you from making bigger decisions with more money on the line early. These early mistakes can be catastrophic. As opposed to the business owner who bootstraps the business initially, who does not have enough money on the line to make big mistakes. They get the luxury of making bigger decisions after they have refined their business skills. Remember, whenever someone says that their business can not be bootstrapped, what they are really saying is that they are not willing to put in extraordinary effort that growing a business will inevitably require.

"Too often we measure everything and understand nothing. The three most important things you need to measure in a business are customer satisfaction, employee satisfaction, and cash flow. If you're growing customer satisfaction, your global market share is sure to grow, too. Employee satisfaction gets you productivity, quality, pride, and creativity. And cash flow is the pulse – the key vital sign of a company."

– JACK WELCH

THAT YOU MUST INVOICE ON CONVENTIONAL TERMS

"94% of invoices take over 30
days to get paid." – Paystone

Business owners often accept conventional invoicing terms as the only way to conduct business. They think they must complete all the work, issue the invoice, and then wait to get paid. Then I find myself meeting with these business owners and discussing their cash crunch, while reviewing their financial statements.

There are several strategies that can be implemented to reduce the burden on waiting for receivables to come in. First, if you can not avoid invoicing, do it more often. Instead of invoicing monthly, do it weekly. Now I am not talking about invoicing weekly if time permits, I am talking about having a rock on your calendar where you invoice even if there is a hurricane passing through town.

The number of times that I am talking to clients who have not been paid because they missed their customers "cut-off" is staggering. Regardless of what they say, your customer is likely prioritizing payments based on a combination of order the invoices were received and how diligent the vendor follows up on that invoice. I do not care if their accounts payable processer calls you to say they normally like it when people bill them every month. Make a visit to that key payable processer to bring them cookies and politely tell them that you bill every week. The regular billing will not only speed up payments to you, but it also has the added advantage of removing timing irregularities on your monthly financial reports.

Then you should look at all opportunities to charge deposits in advance. Even a 10% deposit helps with cash flow and shows that your customer is serious about following through. Often, if charging an advance deposit is not possible, a payment upon start is. For example, if materials are dropped off at the start of the project, the customer will normally be agreeable to paying the entire material cost on day 1. Finally, you want to have a credit card on file, or a third-party financing already approved, so as to facilitate immediate payment on completion whenever possible.

In any event, do not spend time invoicing and collecting small amounts. Businesses often spend more money collecting small invoices, than the invoice is worth. You might have to use some of the tactics above to satisfy key customers. However, anyone who owes you just a couple of hundred dollars is not a key customer. These small customers should have no other options other than paying up front or paying upon completion.

"If the plan is simple
enough, everyone
understands it, which
means each person can
rapidly adjust and modify
what he or she is doing.
If the plan is too complex,
the team can't make rapid
adjustments to it, because
there is no baseline
understanding of it."
– JOCKO WILLINK

THAT YOU NEED EHPENSIVE ACCOUNTING & PROJECT MANAGEMENT SOFTWARE

"85% of employees lose at least one to two hours of productivity a week searching for information." – Dynamic Signal

One of the favourite questions of new entrepreneurs is which fancy industry specific software they should use. It is not unusual, at the point of asking this question, that the entrepreneur has spent more time researching software then doing business with real customers. My answer usually shocks them.

Most of the time this entrepreneur has not even grown to the point where they have actual employees. Thus, I am going to recommend that not only should they forgo the fancy industry specific software, but they do not even need a QuickBooks data file yet. Not only does that surprise new entrepreneurs but most other CPAs would hear that advice and think that I am wrong.

However, I am an entrepreneur first and a CPA second. I know that the single biggest limiting factor is time. Everyone gets 168 hours in a week. I know from studying successful entrepreneurs, that entrepreneurs that build 7 figure businesses spend a disproportionate amount of their time pursing new customers. You should not be wasting time initially overcomplicating the task of tracking a few customers and a few thousand dollars in sales.

The only accounting system you need initiatlly is a dedicated corporate account and a dedicated credit card used exclusively for the business. Simply ensure all the business transactions are reflected in these accounts and ensure personal expenses are not comingled in these accounts. Monitor the activity online weekly, then once a month print out the statements and write notes directly on the statements. Your accountant can take care of the rest at year end. Once you start hiring actual employees other than family members, you are ready to start-up a QuickBooks file. With professional help!

Then the only CRM or project management software you need initiatlly is a free Google Doc or Google sheet. This is going to be foreign for most people starting out because they likely came from a big company with a sophisticated system. However, it is important to remember that the big company you came from likely had dedicated IT people. In a start-up, the IT department and the sales department are one and the same ... you! Thus, any additional IT steals time directly from sales efforts. Create a simple spreadsheet to track customers and schedules. Then get to work selling stuff and do not overthink your simplistic tracking system until you hit a million in sales!

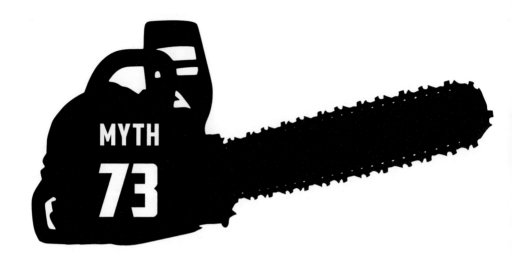

"I am not a product of
my circumstances. I am a
product of my decisions."
– STEPHEN COVEY

THAT BIGGER CUSTOMERS ARE ALWAYS BETTER

"33% of customers say they'll consider switching companies immediately following a single instance of poor service." – American Express

Business owners often lack balance when analyzing the benefits and risks associated with big customers. We often hear about how their business is rock solid because of a relationship with a big customer. Sometimes they feel everything will get easier if they land one big customer.

Big customers can create large profits quickly. Although, there are several risks associated with big customers. First, building a business around a single customer dramatically elevates the risk that your business will eventually fail. Most people read that American Express stat above and immediately think how useful it will be to motivate a team to deliver excellent customer service and that should be the goal. However, despite all your best intentions, things will go wrong.

Some customers will work with you recognizing the value of building long lasting relationships. Sometimes long-lasting relationships evaporate overnight without warning. Over the longer term you must consider retirements and deaths that often end customer relationships. Remember if you are dealing with business customers, 96% of businesses do not last 10 years. Thus, to build your business around a single customer is insane.

Dealing with losing a big customer is far more difficult than dealing with a small customer leaving. Often revenue will take a serious hit, yet your ability to immediately cut some of your costs like rent and wages is often limited in the short term. If you have one of these large customers, at a minimum, you need a contingency plan on how to deal with their exit. You should also remember that the final payment from that big customer is never a sure thing. Your ultimate solution should be to build the customer base to a point where the exit of any one customer does not create the necessity to change directions.

When you come across a big customer you should always give pause before finalizing the deal. Bigger customers often mean covering a bigger payroll and more supplies. Sometimes you must take this leap before ever collecting payment. Thus, you should ask yourself whether you can survive if you do not get paid.

Even if you have the cashflow to support the deal you should consider your time. Sometimes taking on a big customer will detract from the time you have to pursue a plethora of other small customers. This pursuit of indestructible customer diversification should never be put on hold.

"In the long run, managements stressing accounting appearance over economic substance, usually achieves little of either." **– WARREN BUFFET**

THAT YOU NEED A COMPLICATED INCOME STATEMENT

"60% of small business owners feel they are not very knowledgeable about accounting and finance." – Small Business Accounting Report

Almost every client who assembles their own chart of accounts ends up with an income statement with too many accounts. QuickBooks and other popular accounting software make it easy to have one account for office supplies, another for the paper, another for the printer ink, another for the coffee, another for the cleaning supplies, etc.

The assumption being that the more precise the accounts the more efficient you will be at managing your overhead. Most CPAs reinforce this behaviour. After all, they teach us how to do the accounting for big businesses where these specific accounts will have tens of thousands of dollars in them. Thus, justifying their necessity and justifying the cost required to maintain this precision.

Before you know it, the average small business owner has a massive income statement. It is often littered with classification inconsistencies. For example, the ink was a general "office supply" last year and a "printer ink" expense this year. Thus, the analysis as to whether you are being more efficient with overhead expenses usually becomes less clear, the larger the chart of account gets.

The goal of the internal income statement should be to provide a clear summary of the profitability from month to month on a single page. This facilitates quick efficient decision making. This allows the records to be maintained in an efficient manner. Perfect accounting does not increase profitability. Timely, reliable numbers simply allow you to make better decisions. This is what increases your profitability.

Fewer accounts keep you focused on the numbers that matter. It is your understanding of the financial picture as a whole and how that income statement, ties to the balance sheet, and ultimately cash flow, that will determine your probability of success. The detail in overhead accounts has little to do with that outcome. We see time and time again, that unnecessary detail in the income statement is normally negatively correlated with accurate records and business success.

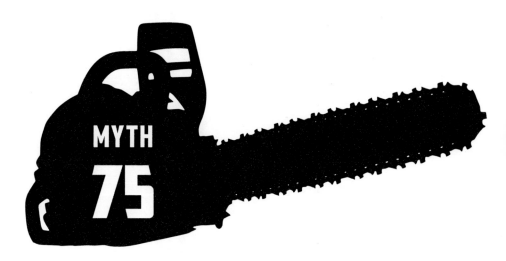

"Simple can be harder than
complex: You have to work
hard to get your thinking
clean to make it simple.
But it's worth it in the end
because once you get there,
you can move mountains."
– STEVE JOBS

THAT YOU CAN AVOID UNDERSTANDING THE BALANCE SHEET

"82% of entrepreneurs scored less than 70% when queried on basic financial literacy questions, such as, balance sheets, accruals, cash flows, etc." – Intuit

When we get to year end or monthly meetings, the clients are always excited to get to the income statement. Sometimes it is almost as if the balance sheet review is an unnecessary or unwanted use of time. I get it, the income statement can be fun. When you are doing well, tracking revenue or income growth can be like watching your favourite sports team score points.

However, I insist that the balance sheet gets reviewed first in the meeting. Reviewing a comparative balance sheet will help identify errors. Any unusual number on the balance sheet has the potential to represent a proportional error on the income statement. Remember, we review the statements first to make good decisions thereafter. Imagine laying someone off you thought unaffordable because of an income statement error that would have been identified with a balance sheet review.

In addition to identify errors, the balance sheet also helps you project cash flow. The income statement could have a ton of revenue, yet all the cash could be tied up in inventory or uncollected accounts receivable. You must know how much profit is required to pay the principal portion of debt each month. The balance sheet tells you all of this.

I often find people trying to assemble complex and highly speculative cash flow projections which are often rendered unnecessary as soon as the business owner learns to interpret the balance sheet. Thus, I encourage questions from the business owners to ensure they understand the amounts and variances between one period and the next. Your expectation should be to receive a simple answer free off technical jargon.

I have learned to trust people who can explain things simply. I have now worked with hundreds of other CPAs throughout my career. I can tell you from experience, that often those who provide highly technical answers, have a just a fleeting understanding of the content. While those who can explain complex transactions simply and concisely tend to understand the material best.

"You don't have to be great
to start, but you have to
start to be great."
– ZIG ZIGLAR

YOU NEED A BIG PERCENTAGE OF THE MARKET

"The North American home renovation market is expected to hit $1.12 trillion in 2025." – Global Newswire

Market research is drilled into people's heads during business school. I often talk to prospective clients who have been working for weeks or months with a government sponsored agency, to research the all-important local market size. Without crushing their spirit, I must let them in on a little secret. Most small business owners, living in a major city, who capture just 1% of their local market, will become the richest person in their entire family!

Let us look at the stat above. If we consider that there are roughly 549 million people in North America at the time of writing, then we can say that the home improvement market in any city of one million people is roughly $2 billion, with a B. Thus, if you are a general contractor and you capture just 1% of that market, you are doing $20 million in revenue each year!

Like many things taught in business school, market research is generally useful for bigger companies. Yet smaller companies spend too much time thinking about it. Partially due to the indoctrination and partially because the alternative is harsher.

The alternative is trying to sell real products and services to real people. Once you do this, harsh truths tend to emerge. Maybe your unique vision to package that product or service does not resonate with real customers outside of flawed market surveys. Maybe although you only need 1% of the market to buy, you have 0% of the market vouching for the quality you bring. Maybe people do not like you. Maybe you can not deal with the inevitable rejection to find out.

I honestly believe that doing market research on a grand scale, before ever selling something to real customers, is like researching high diving techniques before learning to swim. Rather than avoiding the inevitable lion's den of the marketplace just go out and get one no. Then get another no and another. Eventually you will get a yes and then another. Then you will know what the market was looking for. Rarely do you find that the size of that market was your limiting factor.

"Stopping advertising to
save money is like stopping
your watch to save time."
– HENRY FORD

THAT YOU CAN SAVE MONEY BY CUTTING MARKETING

*"60% of businesses that have grown
their profit did so by increasing their
online advertising spend." – BDC*

Most clients look at all expenses as equally negative. They think that the name of the game is to minimize expenses. Minimizing expenses is often good advice for people who earn fixed employment income. As this will provide more money for debt repayment, savings, and wealth creation.

However, businesses by nature do not have fixed income levels. The level of advertising will often directly affect the income generated. Thus, if spending one additional dollar in advertising helps you earn two additional dollars, you should generally do it. As simple as this concept is, it is uncomfortable to believe in because we have been brainwashed into believing that a "penny saved is a penny earned" philosophy, somehow applies to business scenarios without fixed income levels.

Business owners need to fight the primal urge to analyze marketing costs without considering the revenue they can generate. This resolve will normally be further tested as even effective marketing strategies tend to take months to gain any sort of traction.

Even business owners who experience temporary capacity issues should be weary of minimizing marketing expenses. After all, the money you spend on marketing tends to be more closely tied to the revenue you will earn 6 months from now rather than tomorrow. Thus, even if you have temporary capacity constraints you should generally continue your marketing initiatives in perpetuity to avoid future income dips. I find most companies spending less than 2% of their revenue in ads will eventually have a significant decline in revenue due to "bad luck". Conversely the companies with reasonable ad spend have far better "luck".

I was recently reviewing the data from a small-town medical clinic that was considering forgoing the $1,300 per month in radio ads now that their Google ads had gained traction. However, the data was still unclear if the online ads would be sufficient on their own to fill the calendar at the clinic. I advised them to continue with both forms of advertising for not just another month, but another year or so! They were surprised, but I noted that one slow month would cost more than the entire annual budget for the radio ads. Thus, gathering the data of a full year would allow us to gather seasonally adjusted data with relatively low risk.

Remember whichever company in your local area spends the most on ads, is generally at or near the top in terms of market share. The goal should be to spend more on marketing not less.

"You must pay taxes. But
there's no law that says you
gotta leave a tip."
– MORGAN STANLEY

THAT YOU CAN PUT OFF PAYING TAXES

"Over $6 billion in payroll tax penalties
are issued per year." – IRS

Everyone has heard the saying, "there is nothing certain in life except death and taxes". Many people get into business with the knowledge that the tax regimes in most countries, provide favourable treatment for business owners. However, anecdotal knowledge around the tax advantages business owners have over employees, can be dangerous. We find too many business owners come to us after making the mental leap from businesses owners having a tax advantage, to business owners being tax exempt.

This is further complicated that although the government is particularly good at collecting arrears tax balances, they are generally awfully slow to remind you what you owe at any given time. Given the annual tax cycle, it is not unusual for certain balances or entire companies to operate under the radar for a year or more without reminders. However, the tax man eventually comes calling.

If the business owner has nothing saved, they can end up having to pay 2 or more years worth of taxes from a single year of profits. Payroll tax and sales taxes can be worse. These amounts can be larger than the corporate tax and personal tax. Also, they can owe even if the business did not make any money. Thus, catching up on payroll and sales tax is often not just difficult, it can be flat out impossible.

We recommend creating tax plans so that all amounts can be paid in the month they are incurred, rather than the month of filing, or the payment deadline. Some amounts will have to be calculated in real time, other amounts can be reasonably estimated, and a monthly payment can be made based on that estimate.

Most strategies to deal with cash flow constraints by timing tax payments tend to be more hassle than they are worth. Tax deadlines are not like credit cards or lines of credit where the bank is often happy to extend credit in perpetuity so long as you keep paying interest. Government tax collectors can be unpredictable in the terms they will extend. It is not unusual for a business owner to have their entire account frozen should you rub one of these tax collectors the wrong way.

Moreover, paying your taxes in the month they are incurred allows you to view the tax effect within your month end reports. Thus, the tax considerations become more aligned with the day-to-day decisions the business owner makes, rather than an esoteric issue that feels outside of their control.

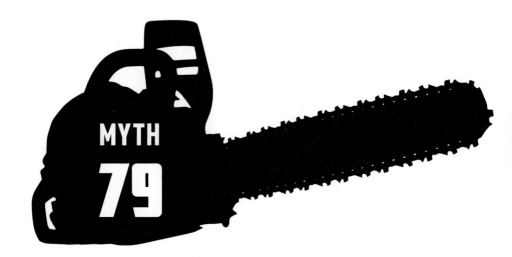

"Stop researching every aspect of it and reading all about it and debating the pros and cons of it ... Start doing it." **– JOCKO WILLINK**

THAT YOU NEED FANCY EQUIPMENT OR LOCATIONS TO START

"33% of businesses get started with less than $5,000 and 58% of businesses get started with less than $25,000." – Smallbiztrends.com

We find a lot of start-ups think that the success of a business is determined by the equipment or location available at start-up. They think that a particular piece of equipment or a particular buildout at a location will make or break their success. We have already discussed how the uncertainty of obtaining a bank loan or an investment may prevent the purchase. However, even if you have the financial wherewithal you should proceed with caution when making significant purchases early on.

First off, fancy locations and equipment will not guarantee that there is any demand for your product or service. Better equipment and locations tend to add capabilities and multiply demand. However, if there is zero demand there is nothing to multiply. There is ordinarily a product skew, in demand within your industry, that will not require significant investment. Further, even if you had the best of the best to start, there is no guarantee that you have the sufficient skills to sell the price points or volumes required to support that overhead. Starting with lower overhead will ensure you understand the industry you are in and ensure your skill set can develop while the costs remain low.

Even business owners with a significant background within their industry tend to dramatically underestimate how much their perspective of best practices changes with ownership. Ask any business owner about a space they built out 5 years later. They will almost always identify significant efficiencies that could have been gained with their new knowledge. Therefore, you should proceed with caution when building out fancy locations upon start-up. Focus on basic and functional.

This extends to equipment. The features you thought were important may be an unnecessary cost. The features you thought were unnecessary could be essential to gain other efficiencies. Thus, I strongly suggest that people consider rented or used equipment to start with.

"Stop focusing on dumb
shit. Don't be afraid to
break things. Don't be
romantic. Don't take the
time to breathe. Don't aim
for perfect. And whatever
you do, keep moving."
– GARY VAYNERCHUK

THAT YOU CAN SPEND SIGNIFICANT TIME ON SMALL OVERHEAD EXPENSES

"74% of overhead is rent & payroll." – Washington Post

We find that most entrepreneurs will spend a disproportionate amount of time on small overhead items. We are taught from an early age that a penny saved is a penny earned. We have probably seen someone in our life negotiate a lower cell phone bill or bank fee. Thus, when cash flow issues arise business owners attempt to fix the cash flow issues by focusing on reducing small more familiar overhead items.

However, businesses rarely fail because of inefficiencies from overhead costs that are normally relatively small in terms of their percentage of revenue. Failing businesses ordinarily have issues with revenue, direct costs, rent, or administrative labour costs. Fixing these items is normally less familiar and less comfortable.

If you have a revenue problem, you generally must focus on generating more leads or increasing the rate at which those leads turn into revenue. Yet, most people have not seen someone in their life redo their sales script or increase their ad spend. If you have a cost of sales problem, you must look at pricing, inventory control, or sourcing new suppliers. All of which are far less familiar than asking for a discount at customer service. Imagine if you are spending too much in administrative labor. Dealing with this problem may lead to a face-to-face conversation where you must lay someone off. Again, most people would rather have a phone conversation with an anonymous banking agent to negotiate fees, rather than lay someone off face-to-face.

Working on the financially significant line items on your financial statement are generally time consuming, scary, and uncertain tasks. Still, you need to avoid tackling insignificant issues just to achieve a false feeling of accomplishment.

Remember every business owner only gets 168 hours in the week. The people who win focus on these big numbers not the small ones. In fact, I find most successful business owners will pay more for suppliers relating to the small overhead items, if they minimize the amount of time spent by the business owner on these issues. It is for this reason that I sort income statements in numerically descending order, with the least significant expenses on the bottom of the page. I literally draw a line in the middle of the income statement and tell business owners to spend all their time above the line working on revenue and the few key expense categories.

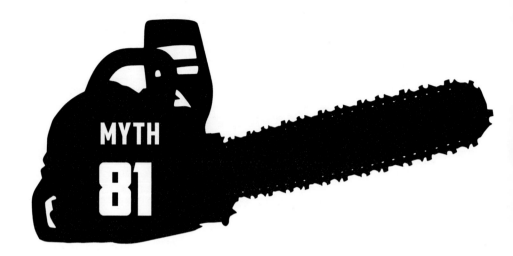

"You do not build a
business, you build people,
and the people build the
business." **– ZIG ZIGLAR**

THAT THE CORPORATION'S PROBLEM, VISION, MISSION, AND VALUES ARE UNIMPORTANT

"71% of workers are 'not engaged' or 'actively disengaged' from their work." – Gallup

Most entrepreneurs, me included, tend to underestimate problem, vision, mission, and values when starting out. Then you will find out that if you ever want to build a team and get them to follow you, these declarations are of utmost importance.

First off, you must be aware that people only buy things to solve problems. Even seemingly frivolous luxury purchases are likely made in the pursuit of perceived lack of fun or status. Thus, if you want to sell things and teach other people to sell your product or services, you need to be clear on the problem you solve.

Then we move into the vision, mission, and values. Before you write these, actively try to unlearn everything you were taught in formal business school. Business school teaches wordy politically correct nonsense that is not memorable. This may be useful for a large corporation pursuing a large percentage of the market who does not want to alienate themselves from large subsets of people. However, most small business owners can become the richest person in their entire families if they capture just 1% of the local market in their chosen field. Thus, it makes little sense to expend extra time trying to bring aboard customers or employees who do not naturally align with you.

The vision should be one line to explain a long-term quantifiable goal. Our vision is to help 1,000 concurrent customers with their businesses. This will take years, given the depth of services we provide for each client. The mission is the purpose you have for each day and the one thing you want employees to filter difficult decisions through. Do not use the terms quality and service. They are overused and not memorable. Our mission is to Help Businesses Beat the Odds. It is concise memorable and unique. Saying you offer high quality service is unmemorable and useless.

Then you should list out your values. Good values will be polarizing. Some employees will read them and run in the other direction. Others will only want to work for your organization and only your organization because of them. Trying to be everything for everyone is a time draining exercise unsuitable for small enterprises.

MYTH 82

"Establishing an effective and repeatable planning process is critical to the success of any team."
– JOCKO WILLINK

THAT EMPLOYEES WILL UNDERSTAND THE MISSION IF YOU EXPLAIN IT ONCE

"2 months after listening to a talk, the average listener will remember only 25% of what was said." – Harvard Business Review

Business owners will often share their frustrations of employee mistakes. However, upon further review the owner is usually at fault.

First off, you must understand the mindset of an employee. They are usually not as passionate about the work as the employer. After all, if they were, they would likely be in business for themselves. Thus, it is not that the employee is dense, it is just that the job represents a small portion of their focus. It is our job as leaders to inspire this focus based on a bold vision.

Also, you must honestly ask yourself after an employee mistake, if you adequately trained them to do the task correctly. Did you invest an hour, 10 hours, 100 hours, or 1,000 hours into training them? Then you must drill further and ask yourself how many times you have reminded them. Was it once, twice, three times, or ten? I would suggest that most employers operate under a misguided view that all employees will do things if they are told once. Even if they have the best of intentions, forgetfulness is the default.

One of the most basic techniques to minimize this forgetfulness is to have standing daily huddles. This allows employees to get instructions and ask questions in a group setting. This allows knowledge to be passed and reminders to be given in a hyper efficient manner. For within that group are multiple people who likely need to be reminded immediately and others who likely have the same challenge soon.

Beyond this you must document best practices. Scripts should be developed for common customer interactions. Written templates should be developed for email or written correspondence. Checklists should be available to navigate workflow and multistep tasks. There should be no ambiguity of expectations for repetitive tasks.

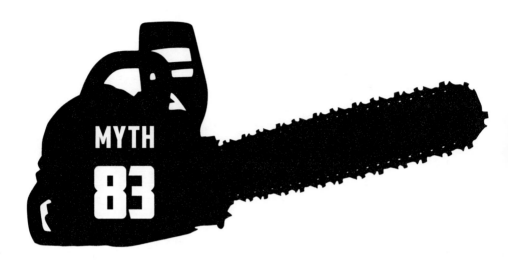

MYTH

83

"Letting the wrong people hang
around is unfair to all the right
people, as they inevitably find
themselves compensating for
the inadequacies of the wrong
people. Worse, it can drive
away the best people. Strong
performers are intrinsically
motivated by performance,
and when they see their efforts
impeded by carrying
extra weight, they eventually
become frustrated."
– JIM COLLINS

EMPLOYEES TELL THE TRUTH ON RESUMES

"85% of all applicants lie on resumes." – Inc.com

We are taught in school that the cornerstone to finding a job is putting together an impressive resume. Unfortunately, in the real-world people shortcut the actual education or experience and often go straight to the writing the resume. Yet we see entrepreneurs devote a disproportionate amount of time in reviewing these works of fiction as a primary means to filter candidates.

Given the rate that people try to dishonestly obtain employment, it becomes clearer as to why the rate of business success is so low. It is incredibly hard to find the right team.

The employer should place far greater emphasis on internally developed aptitude tests and skill tests. Come up with a common task that someone starting out in that role will have to perform. Only offer employment after they have demonstrated proficiency in these tests.

You will find that sometimes those who have less impressive resumes have far more natural aptitude. As you see more and more applicants go through the standardized testing your judgment will dramatically improve. Your ability to see the minute difference between good candidates and great candidates will improve every time you repeat the exercise.

Even after the start date you should have a defined probationary period. Afterall, it is impractical to test every skillset and some people are unable to maintain performance once the daily grind is underway. In any event the quality of new team members goes up, the less you rely on resumes.

"The great majority of
people are wandering
generalities rather than
meaningful specifics."
– ZIG ZIGLAR

YOU CAN FIND GOOD EMPLOYEES BY INTERVIEWING A FEW CANDIDATES

"Google receives 3 million applications per year and only hires 0.2% of the applicants." – CNBC

Business owners often tell me of a prospective hire. They expect me to provide some deep analysis on the applicant's resume and the things they said during the interview. However, my primary question usually surprises them.

I like to ask, how many people did you interview for the position? You can usually count the number on one hand. Extroverted business owners normally generate applicants from contacts over time. Then they tend to overvalue the applicants derived from networking with their contacts. However, 1 applicant from networking is normally just that, 1 applicant. Meanwhile the big businesses you are competing against are interviewing hundreds of applicants or in Google's case millions. Who do you think finds the top talent?

To compete you should make a concerted effort to meet 100 people face to face to hire 1. To make this practical from a time perspective you will normally have to deploy group interviews. As with most effective business strategy, it will likely feel unnatural. Like you are minimizing each applicant's voice. However, you will no longer have to endure the no show applicants and sitting through interviews which you knew are a bad fit in the first 5 minutes. Before you write this strategy off as crazy, remember, big employers like Google, Disney, and the Ritz Carleton use this time hack as well.

The more people you meet, the more you will realize that the best candidates rise to the occasion in this forum. I have often let clients shadow my group interview process. Even though they are not accountants, they pick the same applicant. After all, the cream rises to the top in a group setting and by evaluating everyone at once, you remove the biases that come with our changing energy levels throughout the day.

A weekly group interview will prevent you from having to scramble once you are short handed. If you diligently conduct a weekly group interview, you will likely already have met a suitable staff member when unexpected growth or staff departure occurs. Thus, removing the stress associated with being short handed.

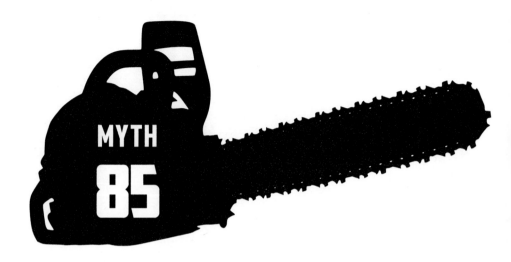

"Don't use a lot where a little will do." – **PROVERB**

THAT INTERVIEW QUESTIONS MAKE BAD CANDIDATES GOOD

"46% of newly hired employees fail within 18 months of being hired." – Forbes

I find entrepreneurs tend to over analyze interview questions. It is like they are constantly looking for some brain teaser question or psychological test that will guarantee the success of a candidate.

These tools can be useful but only as a supplement to more tangible activities. After all, an interview lasts for an hour or two and a successful employee will have to perform for a decade or two.

We talked before about having a group interview that allows you to meet 100 people face to face before hiring one. You should have polarizing vision, mission, and values presented to applicants orally and in writing during the group interview. Successful applicants will clearly be able to articulate why they want to work for your business. Average applicants will only be able to articulate why they want to work in your industry, instead of your business.

The group interview will serve as a forum for motivated employees to return more than once. After all, perseverance is best observed rather than talked about.

Once you are interested in someone, they should have an opportunity to shadow within your organization for an entire day. It is surprising how many people can hold it together for an hour-long interview. However, once you spend a day with them, their true colors tend to shine through. Often, they will reveal their shortcomings to fellow employees. Not knowing that A level employees will gladly report to management on these shortcomings as they do know C level employees will make their jobs more difficult.

If you want to get in touch with each applicant's Freudian qualities in addition to these tangible filters, so be it. However, do not use psychological testing in place of these basic proven techniques.

"Life shrinks and expands
on the proportion of your
willingness to take risks
and try new things."
– GARY VAYNERCHUK

EMPLOYEES WILL STAY FOREVER

"The average millennial stays with an employer for 2.3 years." – United States Bureau of Labour Statistics

We see businesses thrust into complete chaos when a single employee exits the organization. Often complete functions of the business are unknown to anyone else in the organization. Thus, the owner is in a perpetual state of figuring out where the last person left off and training someone new repeatedly.

To get off this doom loop you must come to terms with the fact that employees do not stay forever. Sometimes the entrepreneur's ego will tell them that they have an innate ability to read people. However, let us be real. 50% of marriages end in divorce. How can you possibly predict each time an employee will decide to move on, get sick, or get pregnant? Stop deluding yourself.

It will feel weird as we are taught from an early age that the only virtuous outcomes are lifelong relationships. This is simply not the case. Some should stay forever, and some should move on when their interests move outside of the organizations mission. Ideally, we should be happy for these people when they move on under good terms. Happy but prepared!

As employees will generally exit on their time schedule not yours, you always need to be prepared. Thus, you should start writing checklists and templates to make it easier to train incoming individuals on routine tasks. Also, as your organization grows you should cross train individuals. This allows incoming employees to be trained by existing employees, allowing you to be permanently removed from the training of that task.

Be weary of people within the organization who are resistant to cross training. These are generally people looking to unfairly leverage knowledge of an otherwise repeatable function. They will usually end up looking for excess pay increases, unreasonable amounts of time off, and/or expect others to deal with their lack of decorum. In more serious cases, this can be a primary indicator of theft or fraud.

Cross training also involves ensuring key client relationships are nurtured by more than one individual within the organization. This will allow the client relationship to transition seamlessly. It also minimizes the risk that exiting employees take key clients with them as they leave.

There will come a day where you will have the confidence to never rely on an exiting employee working out their notice. As the post notice work is always done after they have checked out emotionally. Instead, you will shake their hand and transition them out the same day the decision is made.

"Those who build great
companies understand
that the ultimate throttle
on growth for any great
company is not markets, or
technology, or competition,
or products. It is one thing
above all others: the ability
to get and keep enough of
the right people."
– JIM COLLINS

YOU CAN HIRE OUTSIDERS TO FILL KEY POSITIONS

"91% of the CEOs from companies that outperformed the market long term were promoted from within." – Good to Great

Often, we get the smiling client come to our office finally ready to scale their business. They are finally making enough money to hire managerial help and they have resumes from potential candidates. This is the start of one of the most difficult conversations we will have with a client.

The truth is that hiring from the outside for key positions is less likely to work than promoting from within. After all, you generally win in business by differentiating yourself from competitors in a way that appeals to customers. However, the experienced person from the outside is going to feel naturally inclined to take your company backwards towards industry standards, which are inconsistent with your key differentiation factors.

Also, there was likely a unique culture that was a key driver for the initial success. It is far easier to acclimate junior positions to that culture than senior positions. Finding someone with experience who is instantly compatible with that culture is improbable. Thus, friction will likely ensue.

Finally, some junior staff are likely to feel demotivated when they see outsiders come in and leapfrog them within the organization. They may feel that their efforts in helping drive the initial success are underappreciated and begin to question if their continued employment will get them to their personal career goals. Thus, efforts begin to suffer, and turnover is likely to ensue.

The most difficult thing about accepting this truth is the solution is not quick. It involves developing talent from within. It involves paying for employees to take certifications during their employment. Undertaking the cost of having employees shadow roles above their pay grade. It means taking time out on the clock to train and coach employees. It takes years!

Failing to do this early will generally result in a stagnation at a certain revenue level due to lack of promotable talent from within or opening the revolving door of outsiders who tend to turnover like pancakes. Start planning for this now. If it means opening spots on your team by clearing out functional employees with low talent ceilings, for rookies with a higher talent ceiling, so be it.

"It is paramount that
senior leaders explain
to their junior leaders
and troops executing the
mission how their role
contributes to big picture
success." – JOCKO WILLINK

EMPLOYEES WILL ALWAYS BE HAPPY WITH YOU

"The typical manager spends 25-40% of their time dealing with conflicts." - Forbes

Our clients often voice the grievances of their employees during our meetings. It is usually a well meaning briefing in search of a solution that brings perfect harmony.

Often what needs to get done in the short term to win at business is not comfortable. Also, it can be more difficult for the worker to connect short term tasks to long term objectives, than for the owner who cast the vision. Further, it can be uncomfortable for workers to accept strategy from leadership that will inevitably vary from their own from time to time. All of this is further complicated by the fact that human beings are emotional creatures, and those emotions fluctuate daily. Often moods are significantly affected by circumstances completely outside the scope of the workplace.

Thus, a certain amount of conflict is unavoidable. You can seek to minimize it by periodically communicating the organizations vision and tying daily tasks to the vision. You can listen to suggestions. However, in the interest of efficiency you can not afford to engage in an arduous debate every time an employee's opinion diverges from your intended course.

If you ask an employee to do 10 tasks, they will almost certainly hate 1 of them. Similarly, if you ask 10 employees to do the same thing, one of them will think your strategy is faulty. However, the truly faulty strategy would be to wait for 100% buy in before becoming productive.

Constant attention to every grievance tends to perpetuate smaller and smaller issues being brought forward. At the end of the day, running a business is a benevolent dictatorship. Focus your attention first on the goal and secondly on repetitive sources of conflict that have a clear strategy for resolution. Give no time to isolated instances of friction or perpetually upset employees.

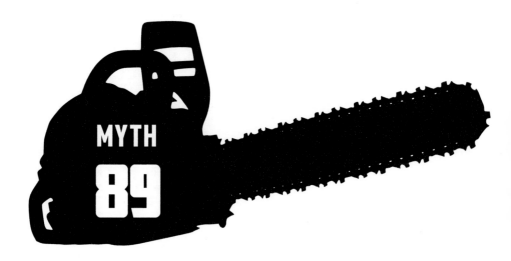

"Most people today are not getting
what they want. Not from their jobs,
not from their families, not from their
religion, not from their government,
and, most important, not from
themselves. Something is missing
in most of our lives. Part of what's
missing is purpose, values. Worthwhile
standards against which our lives can
be measured. Part of what's missing is
a game worth playing."

– MICHAEL GERBER

EMPLOYEES VALUE THEIR RATE OF PAY THE MOST

"Only 12% of employees actually leave their job because they want more money." – CareerBuilder.com

When business owners lose a key staff member, for the first time, they usually falsely blame pay rates. They assume that the main driving force for the employee's departure was because a new employer could afford to pay them more.

Then I start asking the hard questions. Did the employee's values align with the documented polarizing values of the corporation? How often did you spend one on one time with that employee to resolve issues quickly and provide recognition? Was the employee provided a long-term plan within the company that met their career goals? How much did you invest in their training?

Normally, little consideration has been given to these critical issues and the business owner has over emphasized the rate of pay. I believe, as business owners, we are guilty of living in our head and falsely assume that everyone else in our business is in tune with our thoughts. Thus, even though this key person was appreciated and had room to grow within the organization, it never gets vocalized.

I believe most busy business owners put off these important human resource functions because they believe they will be a burdensome formal process. It does not have to be rocket science.

Most business owners would move their company culture forward significantly by simply scheduling a 2-hour time block every week. For the first hour, you train employees or do team building activities. Then the second hour is set aside to meet one on one with employees. You might not meet with every employee every week. However, it gives you time to recognize exemplary performance from the prior week or correct small issues before they become major issues.

These discussions will naturally facilitate discussing the employees hidden challenges and long-term career objectives. Again, this does not have to be an overly formal process. Just get the time block on the calendar and start investing 2 hours per week.

"Creativity dies in an
undisciplined environment."
– JIM COLLINS

THAT AN EMPLOYEE'S SKILL IS AS IMPORTANT AS THEIR ADVERSITY QUOTIENT

"Employees spend approximately 2.8 hours each week involved in a conflict." – CPP Inc.

I find entrepreneurs accept and make too many excuses for underperforming employees. After all, many entrepreneurs start a business because of bad experiences working for other people. Thus, there is a tendency to over accommodate poor performance.

Now I am not saying that you cannot do better than the boss who drove you to go out on your own. However, to win at the sport of business you need people who are mentally tough on your team. As you cannot completely shelter them from adverse circumstances.

Jobs will have to get done when weather is bad. Equipment will break down. Customers will be unreasonable. Suppliers may not always deliver on their promises. Working hours are subject to change.

These are just some of the things related to the actual job. Employees will still have to deal with sickness and injury. Family conflict. Car problems and mechanical failures at home.

Our goal as leaders should be to minimize adverse circumstances but we cannot tolerate people who routinely fail to perform unless circumstances are ideal. Employees with good skills and high amounts of adversity quotient or perseverance, will ordinarily outperform those with excellent skills and low adversity quotient as the years pass.

Thus, we should focus on recruiting and promoting those employees who display high levels of adversity quotient. Remembering that although those with higher skill levels may move faster in ideal situations, they are likely to implode when circumstances inevitably get difficult.

Moreover, we need to set the example of consistency. We need to demonstrate the willingness to engage in difficult conversations. We need to demonstrate resourcefulness when others would give up. We need to be the ones who show up on time even when our cars are in the shop.

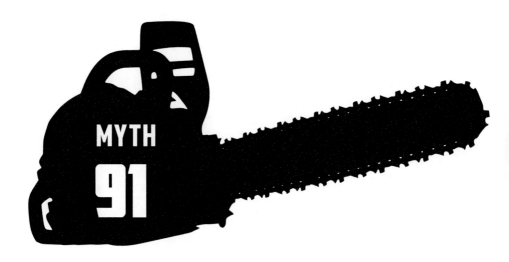

"The goal of all leaders
should be to work
themselves out of a job.
This means leaders must
be heavily engaged in
training and mentoring
their junior leaders to
prepare them to step
up and assume greater
responsibilities."
– JOCKO WILLINK

THAT EMPLOYEE'S PERSONAL GOALS WILL ALIGN WITH THE BUSINESS OBJECTIVES

"40% of departing employees cite lack of future career development." – Global Talent Monitor

Business owners often live in their own head not communicating the vision to their employees. I often hear about the business owners plans for next months sales or a new location in 24 months. However, I find these goals are rarely communicated to the staff.

Moreover, how the employee will mutually benefit from this long-term goal is rarely thought about. After all that new revenue may facilitate a raise and that next location will require promoting someone to manage it. Sadly, the lack of discussion on these goals and the opportunities they create for the entire team, undermines the ability to accomplish those goals.

Employees are stuck wondering how they will ever get a new title, buy a new home, or pay for their kids schooling. As the disconnect between their personal life and the company's objectives grows, they ultimately leave. The most unfortunate part being that achieving the company's goals could potentially facilitate their personal goals, but the connection goes undiscussed.

It is important to carve out time in your calendar each week for one-on-one time with your employees. You might not talk with each one of them each week, but you should not go months without having a heart to heart. Get to know them. Understand their personal objectives. Find ways that their employment can facilitate these objectives. It might mean more training, more pay, or more vacation time. Once identified, identify a company metric that will unlock that perk for them.

Sometimes the discussion itself is all that is required. The employee may have an issue that you have already solved. For example, financing a home, finding childcare, or passing industry related exams. Sharing your experience will save the employee from learning the hard way.

"The Dichotomy of Leadership. A good leader must be: confident but not cocky; courageous but not foolhardy; competitive but a gracious loser; attentive to details but not obsessed by them; strong but have endurance; a leader and follower; humble not passive; aggressive not overbearing; quiet not silent; calm but not robotic, logical but not devoid of emotions; close with the troops but not so close that one becomes more important than another or more important than the good of the team; not so close that they forget who is in charge. Able to execute Extreme Ownership, while exercising Decentralized Command. A good leader has nothing to prove, but everything to prove."

– JOCKO WILLINK

THAT EMPLOYEES WILL DO WHAT YOU HAVE NEVER DONE

"57% of employees have left a job
because of their managers." – DDI
Frontline Leader Project.

When I say that employees will not do what you have never done, I am not saying that you must be proficient in every technical function of your business. As your business grows, you will likely hire people who have more experience or specialized training in a particular area than you do. What I am saying is that you cannot expect employees to a have a higher level of determination than you do.

You can not expect someone to open the shop on time if you are late for appointments. You can not expect someone to preserve through a rigorous training program if you have never done so yourself. You can not expect an employee to go above and beyond for a customer if they have never seen you do it.

The goal over time, is to have this discipline adopted by your managers. Then as the team gets bigger, the employees can rely on the management team to demonstrate a winning work ethic. Thus, facilitating you to work less and less hours as the years go by. However, unless you put in a decade or so to personally instill this culture your dreams of time freedom will likely never come to fruition.

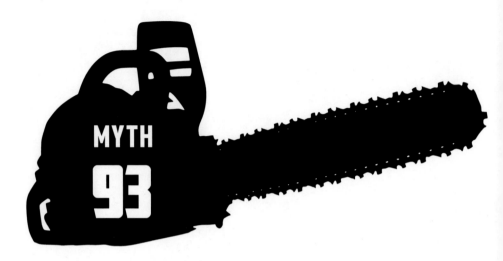

"The basic idea of email
has remained essentially
unchanged since the
first networked message
was sent in 1971. And
while email is great for
one-on-one, formal
correspondence, there
are far better tools for
collaboration."
– RYAN HOLMES

THAT EVERYONE NEEDS THEIR OWN EMAIL

"On average, office workers receive at least 200 messages a day and spend about two-and-a-half hours reading and replying to emails." – Forbes

I have noticed that small businesses tend to overemphasize having unique emails for everyone in the organization. Yet if you want assistance from a big business, they have a single general inquiry email. Do you think the big businesses have not considered issuing more unique email addresses?

Well of course they have. However, they have concluded that that it is far easier to manage fewer email accounts. This allows the inevitable distraction of emails to be siloed into a few individuals as opposed to having every individual in the organization bearing the brunt of this distraction. This prevents high level man hours being spent on administrative tasks. This also allows oversight from a central location.

You should think of managing email as a particular function within your business rather than a function of each employee. Ideally you should isolate yourself, as CEO, and other high-level staff from this function.

Moreover, this will prevent the doom loop of internal emails. One of the biggest time sucks is having internal team members trying to facilitate a back-and-forth communication and collaboration via email, when they are working in the same location. It is usually highly inefficient and given the ambiguity of tone within emails, it often becomes bad for moral. Daily huddles can normally eliminate the need for interoffice emails.

MYTH
94

"We don't like checklists. They can
be painstaking. They're not much fun.
But I don't think the issue here is mere
laziness. There's something deeper,
more visceral going on when people
walk away not only from saving lives
but from making money. It somehow
feels beneath us to use a checklist,
an embarrassment. It runs counter to
deeply held beliefs about how the truly
great among us—those we aspire to
be—handle situations of high stakes
and complexity. The truly great are
daring. They improvise. They do not
have protocols and checklists. Maybe
our idea of heroism needs updating."

– ATUL GAWANDE

THAT IT IS NOT NECESSARY TO TEMPLATE COMMON PHONE AND EMAIL INTERACTIONS

"Central line checklists in Michigan ICU's saved $175 million dollars in 18 months." – Checklist Manifesto

Most business owners that I meet have few or no templates, scripts, or checklists. I believe a lot of entrepreneurs start businesses to get out of the bureaucracy of a big business. However, without standardization you can never train a team and scale.

Running your own business will allow you to avoid unnecessary bureaucracy but you should be prepared to implement time saving standardization whenever possible. After all, the entrepreneurs in charge of the business are often more comfortable with uncertainty than the staff they will hire. Staff tend to value the certainty of checklists. It gives them clarity on what the expectations are and reduces the anxiety associated with making a mistake.

If you are starting from ground zero do not think about the 500-page manual from the corporate job you left. Think about the basics. You should have standardized scripts and questions that you should ask new prospective customers when they call in. You should have templated emails to ask the same should new customers reach out by email. This allows you to invest hours into content, grammar, and even the font. Thus, allowing you to be concise, effective, and demonstrate proficiency.

Then think about the other simple tasks within your organization. Like opening the shop, responding to emails, and confirming appointments. If the work of your staff on a particular task continually differs from your expectations, a script, template, or checklist, is in order. It will increase quality and efficiency

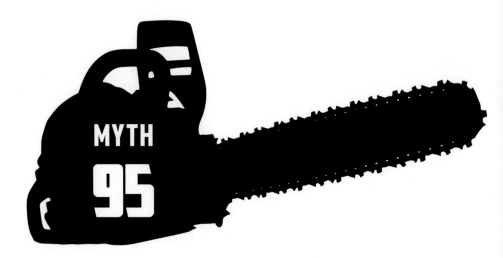

"Good checklists, on the other hand
are precise. They are efficient, to the
point, and easy to use even in the most
difficult situations. They do not try
to spell out everything--a checklist
cannot fly a plane. Instead, they provide
reminders of only the most critical and
important steps--the ones that even the
highly skilled professional using them
could miss. Good checklists are, above
all, practical." **– ATUL GAWANDE**

THAT YOU CAN NOT
CHECKLIST COMPLEX TASKS

"Central line checklists in Michigan ICU's saved 1,500 lives in 18 months." – Checklist Manifesto

Moving beyond the simple checklists I find more skepticism that checklists and templates can aid the complex tasks of a business. The level of education of the business owner is usually negatively correlated with their willingness to accept that checklists will help. After all, if they went for school for 4 to 10 years to do the job, how could a checklist help.

One of our presenters at our Beat the Odds at Business Bootcamp is a master electrician. He has been doing electrical work for decades. He has created a checklist to go through when wiring basement developments. There are over 100 items on his checklist that he shares at the event. It does not matter how long you go to school, remembering 100 items consistently on command is impractical.

Even in our firm we have an annual financial and tax planning checklist that we go through. Financial planning and tax planning is one of the more technical exercises that you do. A qualified CPA who uses this checklist will likely have gone to school for 7 years. Even though I am the person who wrote the checklist, if I were to complete the task without the checklist, I would take more time and make more mistakes.

The checklist is not designed to make a non-electrician a master electrician. It does not make a non-CPA a CPA. It does not make a non-doctor a doctor. It does not make a non-pilot a pilot. They make the electrician a better electrician. They make the CPA a better CPA. They make the doctor a better doctor and the pilot a better pilot.

After all the benefits of a business can only be realized if you build and train a team. The technician with good skills, who can teach average technicians to be great, will normally be more valuable than a technician with excellent skills that can not teach!

"People do not wander
around and then find
themselves at the top of
Mount Everest." **– ZIG ZIGLAR**

THAT YOU CAN NOT COUNT CULTURE

"43% of surveyed employees claim corporate culture was the main reason for their search for a new job." – Hays

Some entrepreneurs can quote the Peter Drucker line that "culture eats strategy for breakfast". Even if they are not aware of the direct quote, people intuitively value culture higher than strategy and systems. However, I would argue that having one without the other is unlikely.

Sure, if you have a team of A players with a strong team culture you will outperform a team of B players with better strategy. Eventually the team of A players will simply recognize and copy a superior strategy. Then they will proceed to outwork and out execute the weaker team.

However, those A players did not come together to build that culture by accident or luck. Do not let your ego fool you into thinking that your innate sense of character recognition will allow you to hire better. The superior culture will not arrive because of your amazing charisma.

The culture arrives because you specifically wrote out the vision, mission, and values that were important to you. You then set out to over communicate it. You did more face-to-face interviews to hire each employee than your competitor. You brought the group together at the beginning of each day more times than your competitors. You did more training sessions to develop talent than your competitors. You did more one to one employee coaching sessions than your competitors.

Although culture will outperform strategy over time, the culture never materializes by accident. You first need a strategy to develop culture. The good ones always take time and effort. You do not have to be Gandhi or Martin Luther King to implement a cultural shift in your business. You just need a unique vision and then begin to count the simple acts of communicating and imparting that vision over time.

"Life is a classroom. Only
those who are willing to be
lifelong learners will move
to the head of the class."
– ZIG ZIGLAR

THAT ANNUAL EMPLOYEE PERFORMANCE REVIEWS ARE USEFUL

"74% of employees feel in the dark about how their managers and peers think they are performing." – Fast Company

Clients often ask me how I do annual performance review. I tell them the truth, I stopped.

Business school reinforced the value of annual reviews. My real-world experience has taught me they are useless. If an employee is underperforming it is highly detrimental to let that go unchecked for weeks never mind a full year. Also, as time passes everyone's recollection of the shortcoming is diminished and thus the debrief is of little quality. Moreover, annual reviews create timing errors. Real world employee performance has ebbs and flows throughout the year. Reviewing performance once a year means that some employees will score too high or too low by placing too much emphasis on recent performance.

The outcome is not better for star performers. They will go without congratulations for up to year. The lack of timely positive reinforcement will likely create a drift back to mediocrity. After all, exemplary performance is likely the result of exemplary effort. The employee has no reason to maintain that effort, if it was not known that it is appreciated. Even worse, that star performer may take another job in search of that appreciation prior to the annual review taking place.

You need time in your schedule to meet one on one with employees every week. You do not have to meet with every employee every week. However, you should prioritize meeting with those needing extra help and those that have gone the extra mile.

I have found that this one-on-one time dramatically reduces the need to fire people and the related legal and emotional consequences. If you bring people into the office every week to tell them about their short comings, they tend to either get in line or get themselves off the bus by quitting. Thus, allowing all parties to move forward knowing they gave it an honest effort.

"Don't try to plan for every contingency. Doing so will only overburden you and weigh you down so that you cannot quickly maneuver."
– **JOCKO WILLINK**

THAT YOU SHOULD MAKE DECISIONS BY CONSENSUS

"There is more media created in 60 seconds than can be consumed in a lifetime." – KPMG

Most entrepreneurs I meet think businesses are democracies. Although the virtues of political democracy are drilled into us during our school years, the virtue is largely irrelevant in business. After all, governments are big slow-moving entities, that only work because their customer can not opt out of paying taxes and they do not need their banker's permission to borrow into eternity. Businesses do not have this luxury.

Putting decisions to a vote grinds decision making to a halt. Thus, removing one of the key advantages that small businesses have over big businesses. Speed! Moreover, the employees are a biased party, in that they ordinarily want to do less and/or be paid more. If you surveyed fast food workers, many would not want to ask every customer to upsize their meal. It is extra work, and it is not enjoyable. However, it is a proven strategy to increase profits. Thus, asking an employee a business strategy question can be a lot like asking a politician who you should vote for.

Moreover, consensus decisions are normally at odds with effective decisions. Let us say you have a restaurant. Half the staff wants to add a steak and steak sauce to a menu. The other half wants to add a salad and a vinaigrette sauce to the menu. Compromising by adding a steak and a vinaigrette sauce to the menu benefits no one.

In most business decisions, there will likely be no profitable solution that pleases everyone. Engaging in endless debate with employees is counterproductive. This does not mean that you should not listen to employees. It just means you need to solicit advice as time permits and when the time comes, be willing to take decisive action without delay, regardless of the popularity.

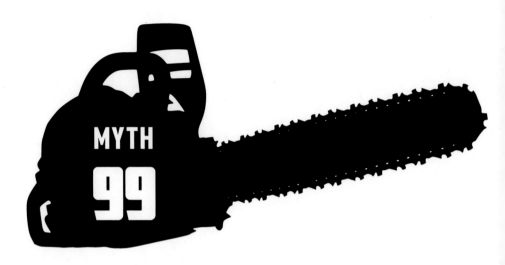

"Life is too short to spend
your precious time trying
to convince a person who
wants to live in gloom and
doom otherwise. Give lifting
that person your best shot,
but don't hang around long
enough for his/her bad
attitude to pull you down.
Instead, surround yourself
with optimistic people."
– ZIG ZIGLAR

THAT YOU CAN AVOID FIRING PEOPLE

"46% of new employees fail within 18 months." – Forbes

In recurring monthly strategy meetings, I often hear about significant friction with a particular employee over and over. The client will almost always look within thinking they have done something wrong. They will ask for suggestions on optimizing pay structure, benefits, or vacation time.

However, if issues with a particular employee keep arising and the relationship with the other staff is good, I know there is likely no advice I can give to salvage the relationship. Eventually that employee will likely leave on bad terms or the client is going to have to bite bullet and fire that employee.

No one likes this answer. Clients will usually sit on a recommendation to fire someone for too long. You should remember that this is your business. Issues are going to crop up here and there, but if a particular employee causes you continual stress, they need to go.

Booking that one-to-one time with staff will minimize the number of issues that rise to a level where someone needs to be fired. Simply holding people accountable each week normally causes incongruent personnel to remove themselves. Thus, absolving you of the uncomfortable part.

That said, you are likely going to have to fire people along the way. Despite the best efforts to select good fits and coach people along. Most bad behaviours are like cancer. If you do not act, they spread to the rest of the team. They even spread to the business owner. If you do not cut out the bad apples, you could end up hating your job, at the company you own!

Firing someone is not as bad as it seems. By making best efforts each week to coach the individual up, you will be able to move forward with a clean conscious. Ultimately the person getting fired may end up somewhere where they are appreciated. Just ask your lawyer and your accountant how to do it with minimal costs and acceptable risk. Remember all decisions carry an element of risk. Then rip off the Band-Aid.

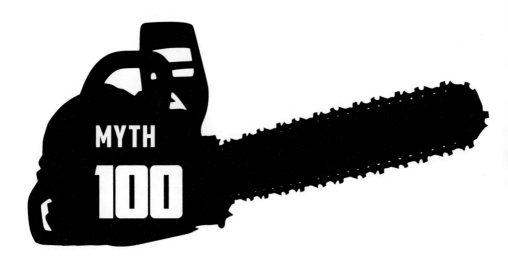

"When you stop planning
and preparing...you stop
winning."
– ZIG ZIGLAR

THAT YOU CAN STOP RECRUITING.

"On average each vacancy will cost a company $500 per day." – Talent Now

Inexperienced entrepreneurs will only tell you that they are hiring when there is an obvious position available. However, if you ask an experienced entrepreneur if they are hiring, they will almost always say yes.

First off, when employees leave, they will almost always leave on their time. Any work done after notice has been given will range from marginal work to a complete waste of time. I have yet to see anyone deliver on an elite level on their way out the door.

Also, the chances that top performers will be available when you have a glaring need is low. There are some employees that are so good that you should make a spot for them regardless of immediate need. However, you will likely never meet these people if you are only looking during times of extreme need.

You should have a permanent ad. You should have a standing weekly group interview and a time efficient way to test skills. The last thing you want to do is saddle yourself or another valued member of your team with hiring responsibilities when you are already short handed.

You want to get to the point where you know the name of your next hire before the next person announces they are leaving. No more notice periods.

Just shake their hand, pay them out, and get them out that day. Business is war. You can not afford to fight it with people about to jump ship or switch sides.

Remember the goal of a business is to grow it. You can not do this without more people. If you stop recruiting, you are essentially betting against yourself. Stop riding your unicycle through traffic. Build a tank!

Are you ready to beat the odds at business?